Teddy Bears& Peanut Soup

Drew Batchelder

a Presidential Trivia and Fact Book

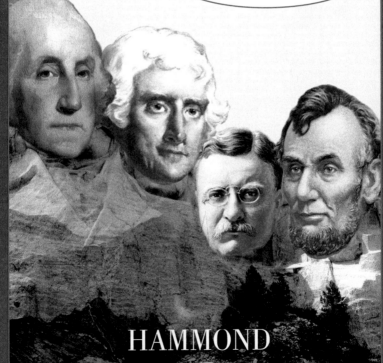

HAMMOND

Acknowledgements

The publisher is very grateful to the invaluable public domain resources available through the Library of Congress, the National Archives, Wikimedia Commons and Google Images. Some of the presidential recipes included in this book are from *A Taste of White House Cooking*, by Arden Davis Melick, published by HAMMOND INCORPORATED © Copyright 1975.

Design and Production:

Hey Kids! Concepts in Education
75 Hudson Street
New York, NY 10013
www.hey-kids.com

Teddy Bears & Peanut Soup
Entire Contents © COPYRIGHT 1975, 1977, 2008 BY
HAMMOND WORLD ATLAS CORPORATION

Based on "The Presidents: Tidbits & Trivia" by Frank, Sidney. Published by Hammond Incorporated in 1975, 1977.

ISBN 978-084-371-638-2
Library of Congress Control Number 2008909934
Printed in Canada

To the Reader

This is a book of unimportant facts about some very important men (and women)! There are *"bear"* facts about **Theodore Roosevelt**, and how a **certain Georgian** got to the White House for peanuts. You will also meet *"Lemonade Lucy," "Princess Alice,"* and the *"Great Bloviator."* **These fascinating, fun, and even funny facts make our 44 Presidents more human and more alive.** Over the past two centuries, the race for the White House has seen a host of entertaining and colorful characters including *"the Rose of Long Island," "His Rotundity,"* and *"the little man on the wedding cake."* The **facts** themselves may seem unimportant, but they bring us closer to the leaders of our great Republic. Besides, you can stump your friends with your new knowledge. And you will learn some interesting *twists* in **American history** while you are at it.

Drew Batchelder

!*!

Contents

Part 3
White House Life

Recipes that will get you to drag out the good china.

White House Recipes.. 117

v

HAVERLY'S MINSTRELS AS THEY APPEARED BY SPECIAL INVITATION AT THE INAUGURATION OF PRESIDENT GARFIELD·

Jimmy Carter
swears in.

Greeks
for
President
Nixon

WHY WE SH

HERBER

TOLD IN TALKI

Is that HH behind the wheel?
Can he drive a stick?

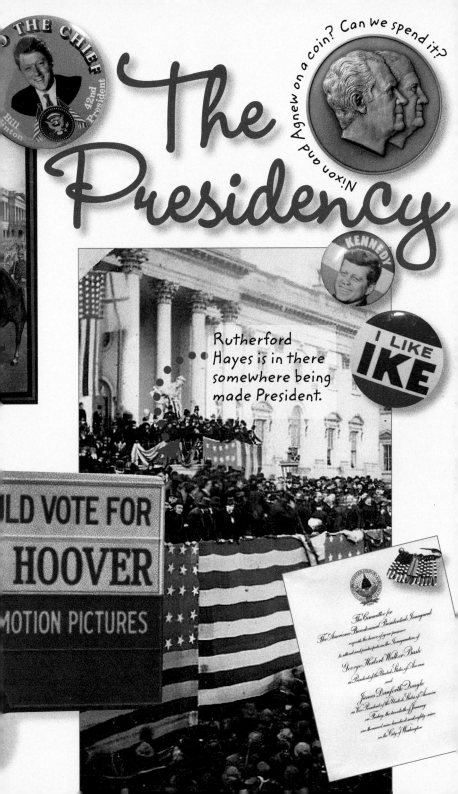

The Presidency

O THE CHIEF

Bill Clinton — 42nd President

Agnew on a coin? Can we spend it?

Nixon and Agnew

KENNEDY

I LIKE IKE

Rutherford Hayes is in there somewhere being made President.

LD VOTE FOR HOOVER MOTION PICTURES

The Committee for
The American Bicentennial Presidential Inaugural
requests the honor of your presence
to attend and participate in the Inauguration of
George Herbert Walker Bush
as President of the United States of America
and
James Danforth Quayle
as Vice President of the United States of America
on Friday, the twentieth of January
one thousand nine hundred and eighty-nine
in the City of Washington

The Presidential Oath

I do solemnly swear* (or affirm)
that I will faithfully execute
the office of President
of the United States,
and will to the best of my ability,
preserve, protect and defend the
Constitution of the United States.

* *Franklin Pierce, inaugurated on Friday, March 4, 1853, was the only President who did not swear. Because of his religious beliefs, he affirmed.*

"When the presidential **bug** gets into your veins," said Senator George Aiken of Vermont, "the only thing that will get it out is embalming fluid."

What's in a Name?

For many years after its creation, the office of **President of the United States** was generally considered to be, and was often called, **Chief Magistrate**. Some of the Founding Fathers favored calling the President "**His High Mightiness.**" Fortunately, this idea never caught on! So how DO you address the President?

"Dear Mr. President,"

An Age of Men

The average life-span of men who have served as President of the United States is 73 years.

Four Presidents lived past their 90th birthdays:
John Adams—90 years, 247 days
Herbert Hoover—90 years, 71 days
Gerald Ford—93 years, 165 days
Ronald Reagan—93 years, 120 days

Six presidents lived past their 80th birthdays:
Thomas Jefferson—83 years, 82 days
James Madison—85 years, 104 days
John Quincy Adams—80 years, 227 days
Harry S Truman—88 years, 232 days
Jimmy Carter—84 years
George Herbert Walker Bush— 84 years

Anniversary Waltz(es)
Nine presidential couples celebrated golden wedding anniversaries.
John and Abigail **Adams**—54 years
John Quincy and Louisa **Adams**— 50 years
Harry and Bess **Truman**—53 years
Dwight and Mamie **Eisenhower**— 52 years
Richard and Pat **Nixon**—53 years
Gerald and Betty **Ford**—58 years
Jimmy and Rosalynn **Carter**—62 years
Ronald and Nancy **Reagan**—52 years
George and Barbara **Bush**—63 years

The oldest man to be inaugurated President of the United States was Ronald Reagan, **69 years old.**

The oldest upon leaving the presidency was Ronald Reagan, who was 77.

The youngest elected President was John Kennedy, 43 at the time of his inauguration.

The youngest President, Theodore Roosevelt, was 42 when he assumed the office following the assassination of William McKinley. (When T. R.'s second term was over, he was still only 50 years old, making him the youngest ex-President.)

The Long and the Short of It

	John Adams	William H. Harrison
	John Quincy Adams	James K. Polk
	Martin Van Buren	Zachary Taylor
	Benjamin Harrison	Millard Fillmore
	William McKinley	Ulysses S. Grant
		Rutherford B. Hayes
		Harry S Truman
James Madison		Jimmy Carter
5 ft. 4 in.	**5 ft. 6 in. — 5 ft. 8 in.**	**5 ft. 8 in. – 5 ft. 10 in.**

But Who's Counting...

Presidents elected without receiving a popular majority:

John Quincy Adams (1824), **James K. Polk** (1844), **Zachary Taylor** (1848), **James Buchanan** (1856), **Abraham Lincoln** (1860), **Rutherford B. Hayes** (1876), **James A. Garfield** (1880), **Grover Cleveland** (1884, 1892), **Benjamin Harrison** (1888), **Woodrow Wilson** (1912, 1916), **Harry S Truman** (1948), **John F. Kennedy** (1960), **Richard M. Nixon** (1968), **James E. Carter** (1976), and **George W. Bush** (2000).

On four occasions, the winning candidate in the popular vote was the loser in a presidential election.

1824: **Andrew Jackson** received 151,271 votes and **John Quincy Adams** 113,122.
Winner: Adams
Reason: *Jackson had not obtained a majority of electoral votes, so the election went to the House of Representatives.*

1876: Samuel Tilden had 4,288,546 votes and **Rutherford B. Hayes** 4,034,311.
Winner: Hayes
Reason: *19 electoral votes were contested (Florida's 4, Louisiana's 8, and South Carolina's 7). A Republican Congress established a special electoral commission. The commission voted, eight to seven, to give the votes to Republican Hayes.*

1888: 5,543,488 people voted for **Grover Cleveland**, and 5,443,892 for **Benjamin Harrison**.
Winner: Harrison
Reason: *Although Harrison had a smaller number of popular votes, he had a total of 233 electoral votes, while Cleveland had a total of 168.*

2000: 50,996,000 people voted for Al Gore, and only 50, 465,000 for George W. Bush.
Winner: Bush
Reason: *The United States Supreme Court stopped the Florida vote recount, in effect awarding Florida's contested electoral votes to Bush.*

5 ft. 10 in. – 6 ft.	6 ft. – 6 ft. 2 in.	6 ft. 2 in. and over
Franklin Pierce Andrew Johnson Grover Cleveland Theodore Roosevelt Woodrow Wilson Calvin Coolidge Herbert Hoover Dwight Eisenhower Richard Nixon George W. Bush	James Monroe Andrew Jackson John Tyler James Buchanan James Garfield William Howard Taft Warren Harding John F. Kennedy Gerald Ford Ronald Reagan Barack Obama	George Washington Thomas Jefferson Abraham Lincoln Chester Arthur Franklin D. Roosevelt Lyndon Johnson George H.W. Bush William Clinton

What's Better than Vice?

One of **Franklin Roosevelt's** vice presidents, Texan John Nance Garner, said that the vice presidency **"wasn't worth a bucket of warm spit."** Reporters are alleged to have cleaned up the spelling of that last word!

On the other hand **nine** former **Vice-Presidents** of the United States were later elected President. They were:
**John Adams
Thomas Jefferson
Martin Van Buren
Theodore Roosevelt
Calvin Coolidge
Harry S Truman
Lyndon Johnson,
Richard M. Nixon
George H.W. Bush**

Presidential Pets

The most common White House pets are cats and dogs. However, some of our presidents have had odder pets. **John Quincy Adams** kept an American **alligator**, and **Herbert Hoover** kept two! **Thomas Jefferson** kept two **bear cubs** while **Martin Van Buren** (briefly!) kept two **tiger cubs**!

Several presidents have had **parrots** for company, but **James Buchanan** had an **eagle**. **Calvin Coolidge** had a **pygmy hippo** and a large variety of other pets. The family of **Theodore Roosevelt** takes the honors, however. They kept —in addition to **eight dogs**—a rat, a pig, a badger, a garter snake (named Emily), ponies, guinea pigs, a hen, and a one-legged rooster!

Presidential School Days

diploma

College Graduates	College Attended
J. Adams	Harvard
J. Q. Adams	Harvard
T. Roosevelt	Harvard
F. D. Roosevelt	Harvard
Kennedy	Harvard
Jefferson	William and Mary
Tyler	William and Mary
Madison	Princeton
Wilson	Princeton
Grant	West Point
Eisenhower	West Point
Polk	North Carolina
Pierce	Bowdoin
Buchanan	Dickinson
Hayes	Kenyon
Garfield	Williams
Arthur	Union
B. Harrison	Miami (Ohio)
Taft	Yale
G.H.W. Bush	Yale
G.W. Bush	Yale
Harding	Ohio Central
Coolidge	Amherst
Hoover	Stanford
L. Johnson	Southwest Texas State
Nixon	Whittier
Ford	Michigan
Carter	Annapolis
Reagan	Eureka College
Clinton	Georgetown
Obama	Columbia

Graduated from Law School	Law School
Hayes	Harvard
Taft	Cincinnati
Wilson	Univ. of Virginia
Nixon	Duke
Ford	Yale
Clinton	Yale
Obama	Harvard

Didn't go to College

Washington	Lincoln
Jackson	A. Johnson
Van Buren	Cleveland
Taylor	Truman
Fillmore	

Attended but didn't graduate

Monroe	William and Mary
W. H. Harrison	Hampden-Sydney
McKinley	Allegheny

Kappa-ing Their Success

Three Presidents were elected to Phi Beta Kappa for their academic performance as college under-graduates: **John Quincy Adams**, Bachelor of Arts, Harvard College, Class of 1787; **Chester A. Arthur**, Bachelor of Arts, Union College (Schenectady, NY), Class of 1848; **Theodore Roosevelt**, Bachelor of Arts, Harvard University, Class of 1880.

White House Obituaries

A compendium of unfortunate demises which occurred during presidential terms of office

Presidents

ASSASSINATIONS

	Date of Occurrence	Died	Age	Served as President
Lincoln	4/14/1865	4/15/1865	56	4 years, 42 days
Garfield	7/2/1881	9/19/1881	49	199 days
McKinley	9/6/1901	9/14/1901	58	4 years, 194 days
Kennedy	11/22/1963	11/22/1963	46	2 years, 306 days

NATURAL CAUSES

	Died	Age	Served as President
W.H. Harrison	4/4/1841	68	30 days
Taylor	7/9/1850	65	1 year, 127 days
Harding	8/2/1923	57	2 years, 151 days
F.D. Roosevelt	4/12/1945	63	12 years, 39 days

First Ladies

	Husband's Term	Died	Age
Letitia Tyler (Mrs. John)	4/6/1841 – 3/3/1845	9/10/1842	51
Caroline Harrison (Mrs. Benjamin)	3/4/1889 – 3/3/1893	10/25/1892	60
Ellen Wilson (Mrs. Woodrow)	3/4/1913 – 3/3/1921	8/6/1914	54

Children

	Parents	Father's Term	Died	Age
Charles Adams	John & Abigail	1797–1801	11/30/1800	20
Mary Jefferson	Thomas & Martha	1801–1809	4/17/1804	25
William W. Lincoln	Abraham & Mary	1861–1865	2/20/1862	11
Calvin Coolidge, Jr.	Calvin, Sr. & Grace	1923–1929	7/7/1924	16
Patrick B. Kennedy	John & Jacqueline	1961–1963	8/9/1963	2 days

The Price of the Presidency

Benjamin Franklin thought the President should receive no salary at all. He made that proposal to the Constitutional Convention in 1787.

The good Doctor Franklin was listened to respectfully and his proposal ignored. Terms of presidential compensation were agreed upon. Through the years, these have changed. Here are the salaries and fringe benefits as they were altered over the years.

PRESIDENTIAL SALARIES

	Annual Amount	Adjusted Value (in 2008 dollars)
1789 – 1873		
	$25,000 salary	**$566,000**
1873 – 1909		
	$50,000 salary	**$865,000**
1909 – 1949		
	$75,000 salary (taxable)	**$1,714,000**
	+ $25,000 travel allowance (nontaxable)	
1949 – 1969		
	$100,000 salary (taxable)	**$875,000**
	+ $40,000 travel and entertainment allowance (nontaxable)	
	+ $50,000 expense account (taxable)	
1969 – 2001		
	$200,000 salary (taxable)	**$1,135,000**
	+ $40,000 travel and entertainment allowance (nontaxable)	
	+ $50,000 expense account (taxable)	
2001 –		
	$400,000 salary (taxable)	**$471,000**
	+ $40,000 travel and entertainment allowance (nontaxable)	
	+ $50,000 expense account (taxable)	

RETIREMENT BENEFITS

Annual pension—$60,000

Office and staff expenses —$96,000

Civil Service retirement benefits—up to $18,000/yr.

Free office space

Free mailing privileges

Free use of government planes

Secret Service Protection

Widow's annual pension —$20,000

You Can't Take It With You

What the Presidents were worth when they died, keeping in mind that:

    A. *There is no information on certain presidents who considered it their own damn business.*

    B. *A dollar is not what it once was, if it ever was.*

Broke	$25,000 - $100,000	$100,000 - $500,000
Thomas Jefferson	**John Adams**	**James K. Polk**
James Monroe	**John Quincy Adams**	**Zachary Taylor**
William Henry Harrison	**Franklin Pierce**	**Grover Cleveland**
Ulysses S. Grant*	**Abraham Lincoln**	**Benjamin Harrison**
	Andrew Johnson	**William McKinley**
		William Howard Taft
		Warren Harding

* *Grant made $500,000 from his Civil War memoirs, but he died before the book was published.*

$500,000 - $1,000,000	Over $1,000,000	Estate not known
George Washington	**Herbert Hoover**	**James Madison**
Theodore Roosevelt	**Franklin Roosevelt**	**Andrew Jackson**
Woodrow Wilson	**John F. Kennedy**	**Martin Van Buren**
Calvin Coolidge	**Lyndon Johnson**	**John Tyler**
Harry S Truman		**Millard Fillmore**
Dwight Eisenhower		**James Buchanan**
		Rutherford B. Hayes
		James Garfield
		Chester Arthur

Surprising Facts

A study by the Urban Institute ranked 20th century Presidents by the amount of the GDP, Gross Domestic Product, they spent on domestic programs. The surprising results? The **biggest spenders** were three Republicans: **Richard Nixon**, **Herbert Hoover**, and **Dwight Eisenhower**! The next two in order were **Harry S Truman** and **George H.W. Bush**. Much more of a surprise, guess who spent the **smallest** percentage of the GDP: **Franklin Delano Roosevelt**!

Hey! How come everyone thought I was cheap?

Herbert Hoover

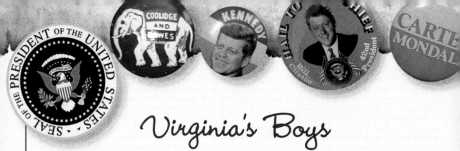

Virginia's Boys

Virginia is known as the **Mother of Presidents**. Eight of Virginia's boys became Presidents of the United States: **George Washington**, **Thomas Jefferson**, **James Madison**, **James Monroe**, **William Henry Harrison**, **John Tyler**, **Zachary Taylor**, and **Woodrow Wilson**. The first four were known as *"the Virginia Dynasty."*

A close second goes to **Ohio**, the birthplace of seven Presidents: **Ulysses Grant**, **Rutherford B. Hayes**, **James Garfield**, **Benjamin Harrison**, **William McKinley**, **William Howard Taft**, and **Warren Harding**.

I Have a Mountain of Work Out There

Mount Rushmore, in the middle of the Black Hills of South Dakota, was a 6,000-foot mountain. A group of locals saw possibilities and linked up with **John Gutzon Borglum**, a rugged and original sculptor. Borglum proposed to carve the granite east face of the mountain into four stone portraits of major Presidents. On the 300-foot perpendicular slab, he wanted to carve (or actually blast and drill):

1. **George Washington** for gaining American independence and establishing the Republic,

2. **Thomas Jefferson** for the Louisiana Purchase, and the opening of the West,

3. **Abraham Lincoln** for saving the American Union,

4. **Theodore Roosevelt** because of that President's enthusiasm and vigor.

Each face is as high as a five-story building (about 60 feet from chin to top of head). **The pupils of the eyes are 4 feet across** and the mouths are 18 feet wide. After Borglum made models, most of the work was done by a crew using pneumatic drills and dynamite. They removed a total of 450,000 tons of stone, and Borglum was justly proud of the fact that not one of them was killed doing it.

The project took **14 years**—from 1927 to 1941. But only 6½ of those years involved real sculpting. The rest of the time sculptor and supporters worked to raise the funds needed to pay for the work. The final cost was about $990,000. Gutzon Borglum died in 1941, just before the work was finished. It was completed by his son, Lincoln.

Accustomed to that Face

United States **currency** features **portraits** of American **Presidents**. The bills in widest circulation favor the more famous faces. The higher they go, the less well-known they become. So a McKinley is worth 500 Washingtons. Perhaps it is ominous to note that banknotes took on their current faces in 1929.

The greenback picture gallery includes:

$1 bill—**George Washington**

$2 bill—**Thomas Jefferson**

$5 bill—**Abraham Lincoln**

$20 bill—**Andrew Jackson**

$50 bill—**Ulysses S. Grant**

Still in use as legal tender but no longer being printed are:

$500 bill—**William McKinley**

$1,000 bill—**Grover Cleveland**

$5,000 bill—**James Madison**

$100,000 bill—**Woodrow Wilson**

There are also **three non-Presidents** that fit the bills: *Alexander Hamilton* (first Treasury Secretary) on the $10 bill, *Benjamin Franklin* (oh, come on! Everybody knows him!) on the $100 bill, and *Salmon P. Chase* (Civil War Secretary of the Treasury) on the $10,000 bill.

Portraits of Presidents also grace United States coins.

The **Lincoln** penny (1909),

The **Jefferson** nickel (1938),

The **Roosevelt** dime (1946),

The **Washington** quarter (1932),

The **Kennedy** half-dollar (1964),

The **Eisenhower** silver dollar (1971) is no longer being stamped.

The US has also tried **Susan B. Anthony**, **Sacajawea** and, more recently, the Presidents but Americans are just not buying dollar coins!

Hey! What about me? I'm the mother of this country!

Martha Washington had her own Silver Certificate!

ALASKA:
Seattle WA to
Fairbanks AL
1,522 miles

Ronald Reagan:
A-OK in
California

HAWAII:
San Diego CA
to Honolulu HI
2,611 miles

	PRESIDENT	BIRTHPLACE	PLACE OF BURIAL
1	Washington	Wakefield VA	Mount Vernon VA
2	J. Adams	Braintree MA	Quincy MA
3	Jefferson	Albemarle Cty VA	Monticello VA
4	Madison	Port Conway VA	Montpelier VA
5	Monroe	Westmoreland Cty VA	Richmond VA
6	J.Q. Adams	Braintree MA	Quincy MA
7	Jackson	Waxhaw SC	Hermitage TN
8	Van Buren	Kinderhook NY	Kinderhook NY
9	W.H. Harrison	Berkeley VA	North Bend OH
10	Tyler	Greenway VA	Richmond VA
11	Polk	Pineville NC	Nashville TN
12	Taylor	Orange Cty VA	Louisville KY
13	Fillmore	Locke NY	Buffalo NY
14	Pierce	Hillsboro NH	Concord NH
15	Buchanan	Franklin Cty PA	Lancaster PA
16	Lincoln	Hardin Cty KY	Springfield IL
17	A. Johnson	Raleigh NC	Greeneville TN
18	Grant	Point Pleasant OH	New York City NY
19	Hayes	Delaware OH	Fremont OH
20	Garfield	Orange OH	Cleveland OH
21	Arthur	Fairfield VT	Albany NY
22 & 24	Cleveland	Caldwell NJ	Princeton NJ
23	B. Harrison	North Bend OH	Indianapolis IN
25	McKinley	Niles OH	Canton OH
26	T. Roosevelt	New York City NY	Oyster Bay NY
27	Taft	Cincinnati OH	Arlington VA
28	Wilson	Staunton VA	Washington DC
29	Harding	Blooming Grove OH	Marion OH
30	Coolidge	Plymouth VT	Plymouth VT
31	Hoover	West Branch IA	West Branch IA
32	F. D. Roosevelt	Hyde Park NY	Hyde Park NY
33	Truman	Lamar MO	Independence MO
34	Eisenhower	Denison TX	Abilene KS
35	Kennedy	Brookline MA	Arlington VA
36	L. Johnson	Stonewall TX	Stonewall TX
37	Nixon	Yorba Linda CA	Yorba Linda CA
38	Ford	Omaha NE	Grand Rapids MI
39	Carter	Plains GA	—
40	Reagan	Tampico IL	Simi Valley CA
41	G.H.W.Bush	Milton MA	—
42	Clinton	Hope AR	—
43	G.W. Bush	New Haven CT	—
44	B. Obama	Honolulu HI	—

Our Presidents:
Birthplaces and Places of Burial

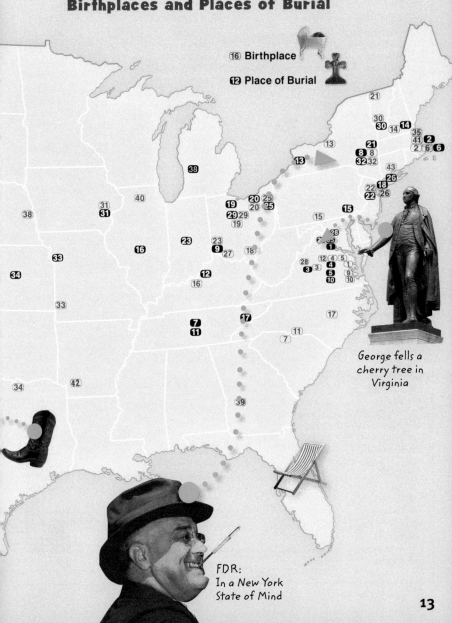

16 Birthplace

12 Place of Burial

George fells a cherry tree in Virginia

FDR:
In a New York
State of Mind

13

Fast Facts About the Presidents

	President	Party	Vice President	Term
1	Washington	Federalist	John Adams	1789-1797
2	J. Adams	Federalist	Thomas Jefferson	1797-1801
3	Jefferson	Democratic-Republican	Aaron Burr/George Clinton	1801-1809
4	Madison	Democratic-Republican	George Clinton/Elbridge Gerry	1809-1817
5	Monroe	Democratic-Republican	Daniel Tompkins	1817-1825
6	J.Q. Adams	Democratic-Republican	John C. Calhoun	1825-1829
7	Jackson	Democratic	John Calhoun/Martin Van Buren	1829-1837
8	Van Buren	Democratic	Richard Johnson	1837-1841
9	W.H. Harrison	Whig	John Tyler	1841-1841
10	Tyler	Whig	(none)	1841-1845
11	Polk	Democratic	George Dallas	1845-1849
12	Taylor	Whig	Millard Fillmore	1849-1850
13	Fillmore	Whig	(none)	1850-1853
14	Pierce	Democratic	William King	1853-1857
15	Buchanan	Democratic	John Breckinridge	1857-1861
16	Lincoln	Republican	Hannibal Hamlin/Andrew Johnson	1861-1865
17	A. Johnson	National Union	(none)	1865-1869
18	Grant	Republican	Schuyler Colfax/Henry Wilson	1869-1877
19	Hayes	Republican	William Wheeler	1877-1881
20	Garfield	Republican	Chester Arthur	1881-1881
21	Arthur	Republican	(none)	1881-1885
22	Cleveland	Democratic	Thomas Hendricks	1885-1889
23	B. Harrison	Republican	Levi Morton	1889-1893
24	Cleveland	Democratic	Adlai Stevenson	1893-1897
25	McKinley	Republican	Garret Hobart/Theodore Roosevelt	1897-1901
26	T. Roosevelt	Republican	(none)/Charles Fairbanks	1901-1909
27	Taft	Republican	James Sherman	1909-1913
28	Wilson	Democratic	Thomas Marshall	1913-1921
29	Harding	Republican	Calvin Coolidge	1921-1923
30	Coolidge	Republican	(none)/ Charles Dawes	1923-1929
31	Hoover	Republican	Charles Curtis	1929-1933
32	F.D. Roosevelt	Democratic	J. Garner/H. Wallace/ H. Truman	1933-1945
33	Truman	Democratic	(none)/Alben Barkley	1945-1953
34	Eisenhower	Republican	Richard Nixon	1953-1961
35	Kennedy	Democratic	Lyndon Johnson	1961-1963
36	L. Johnson	Democratic	(none)/Hubert Humphrey	1963-1969
37	Nixon	Republican	Spiro Agnew/Gerald Ford	1969-1974
38	Ford	Republican	Nelson Rockefeller	1974-1977
39	Carter	Democratic	Walter Mondale	1977-1981
40	Reagan	Republican	George H.W. Bush	1981-1989
41	G.H.W. Bush	Republican	James Danforth (Dan) Quayle	1989-1993
42	Clinton	Democratic	Albert Gore	1993-2001
43	G.W. Bush	Republican	Richard Cheney	2001-2009
44	Obama	Democratic	Joseph Biden	2009-

Born	Died	Zodiac Sign	Wife
02/22/1732	12/14/1799	Pisces	Martha Dandridge Custis
10/30/1735	07/04/1826	Scorpio	Abigail Smith
04/13/1743	07/04/1826	Aries	Martha Wayles Skelton
03/16/1751	06/28/1836	Pisces	Dolley Payne Todd
04/28/1758	07/04/1831	Taurus	Elizabeth Kortwright
07/11/1767	02/23/1848	Cancer	Louisa Johnson
03/15/1767	06/08/1845	Pisces	Rachel Donelson Robards
12/05/1782	07/24/1862	Sagittarius	Hannah Hoes
02/09/1773	04/04/1841	Aquarius	Anna Symmes
03/29/1790	01/18/1862	Aries	Letitia Christian/Julia Gardiner
11/02/1795	06/15/1849	Scorpio	Sarah Childress
11/24/1784	07/09/1850	Sagittarius	Margaret Smith
01/07/1800	03/08/1874	Capricorn	Abigail Powers
11/23/1804	10/08/1869	Sagittarius	Jane Appleton
04/23/1791	06/01/1868	Taurus	*NEVER MARRIED*
02/12/1809	04/15/1865	Aquarius	Mary Todd
12/29/1808	07/31/1875	Capricorn	Eliza McCardle
04/27/1822	07/23/1885	Taurus	Julia Dent
10/04/1822	01/17/1893	Libra	Lucy Webb
11/19/1831	09/19/1881	Scorpio	Lucretia Rudolph
10/05/1829	11/18/1886	Libra	Ellen Herndon
03/18/1837	06/24/1908	Pisces	Frances Folsom
08/20/1833	03/13/1901	Leo	Caroline Scott
03/18/1837	06/24/1908	Pisces	Frances Folsom
01/29/1843	09/14/1901	Aquarius	Ida Saxton
10/27/1858	01/06/1919	Scorpio	Alice Lee/Edith Carow
09/15/1857	03/08/1930	Virgo	Helen Herron
12/28/1856	02/03/1924	Capricorn	Ellen Axson/ Edith Bolling Galt
11/02/1865	08/02/1923	Scorpio	Florence Kling De Wolfe
07/04/1872	01/05/1933	Cancer	Grace Goodhue
08/10/1874	10/20/1964	Leo	Lou Henry
01/30/1882	04/12/1945	Aquarius	Anna Eleanor Roosevelt
05/08/1884	12/26/1972	Taurus	Elizabeth Wallace
10/14/1890	03/28/1969	Libra	Mary (Mamie) Doud
05/29/1917	11/22/1963	Gemini	Jacqueline Bouvier
08/27/1908	01/22/1973	Virgo	Claudia (Lady Bird) Taylor
01/09/1913	05/22/1994	Capricorn	Thelma (Pat) Nixon
07/14/1913	12/26/2006	Cancer	Elizabeth Bloomer
10/01/1924	——	Libra	Rosalynn Smith
02/06/1911	06/05/2004	Aquarius	Anne (Nancy) Davis
06/12/1924	——	Gemini	Barbara Pierce
08/19/1946	——	Leo	Hillary Rodham
07/06/1946	——	Cancer	Laura Welch
08/04/1961	——	Leo	Michelle LaVaughn Robinson

George Washington

Born: *Wakefield VA, February 22, 1732*
Died: *Mount Vernon VA, December 14, 1799*

The Father of His Country

Plenty of Collateral, though...

George Washington owned land in Virginia, Maryland, Pennsylvania, Kentucky, in the Northwest Territory, and in Washington, D. C. —thousands and thousands of acres in all. And yet in March of 1789, Washington had to **borrow** £600 to clean up some debts and to pay for a trip to New York City for his inauguration as President, a ceremony they couldn't very well hold without him.

The First

The first President to receive an **honorary degree** was also our first President. **George Washington** was awarded a Doctor of Laws by Harvard in 1776.

Dogged by His Loss...

The Battle of Germantown in October of 1777 was not just another **American defeat**. It left the Patriot capital city of Philadelphia wide open to British occupation. In the midst of his many troubles, **George Washington** was told that British General William Howe's **dog** had been recovered wandering around the battlefield. It must have pleased, and perhaps even amused, Washington to return the dog with the following note, *"General Washington's compliments to General Howe. He does himself the pleasure to return him a dog, which accidentally fell into his hands, and by the inscription on the Collar, appears to belong to General Howe."*

Thanks, George!

George Washington proclaimed Thursday, November 26, 1789, the **first** national **Thanksgiving Day**.

A Wager Better Lost

During the Constitutional Convention in Philadelphia in 1787, Alexander Hamilton **bet** Gouverneur Morris that Morris would not dare to presume upon the reserved and aloof **George Washington**. Morris took the bet. His **prize** was to be a full supper, complete with wine for Morris and a dozen of his friends.

On the evening appointed, his co-conspirators watched Morris advance beaming on Washington. Morris bowed, shook hands and laid his left hand on the General's shoulder as he exclaimed, *"My dear General, how happy I am to see you look so well."* (The very words proposed by Hamilton when making the bet.)

Washington stepped back and stared icily, silently, at Morris for some minutes. Morris, deeply embarrassed, withdrew to the company of the other bettors.

That evening, at the supper Hamilton provided to pay off his wager, Morris said firmly, *"I have won my bet, but paid dearly for it, and nothing would induce me to repeat it!"*

Right from the Horse's Mouth

All of his life, **George Washington** suffered with **bad teeth**. He tried various dentists and a wide variety of false teeth (made from **hippopotamus** and cow bone, ivory, and even his own teeth). His teeth were a misery. Perhaps that is why he had the teeth of his six white carriage horses brushed every single day!

A Boy's Best Friend

During the American Revolution, **George Washington** sent one of his junior officers to a local landowner to take the **horses** for his officers. The elderly mistress of the plantation was not impressed. *"I have come on the orders of the government,"* the young officer protested. *"On the orders of General George Washington."* The old lady smiled at the young man, *"You go back and tell General George Washington that his **mother** says he cannot have her horses."*

19

Born: *Braintree (now Quincy) MA,*
October 30, 1735
Died: *Quincy MA, July 4, 1826*

The Father of the American Navy

Presidents on the Presidency

66 **No man who ever held the office of President would congratulate a friend on obtaining it.** 99

— **John Adams**

The First

The first President to be the **father** of another President was **John Adams, John Quincy Adams'** father. Later, President **George H.W. Bush** was father to President **George W. Bush**.

JQ

Father's Day

John Adams is called the *"Father of the American Navy."* He introduced a bill in the Continental Congress in October of 1775. The bill provided for the construction of naval vessels to defend the interests of the infant American Republic. October 13, 1775, is regarded as the birthday of the American Navy.

I'll Give You Three Reasons...

Thomas Jefferson was reluctant to write the Declaration of Independence, feeling that **John Adams** was better qualified. Adams thought Jefferson should be the author and told him why:

1 **"Reason first:**
*You are a **Virginian**, and Virginia ought to appear at the head of this business.*

2 **"Reason second:**
*I am **obnoxious**, suspected and unpopular; you are very much otherwise.*

3 **"Reason third:**
*You can **write** 10 times better than I can."*

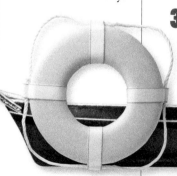

Don't Get No Respect

John Adams was very short and, with age, he became quite chubby. Behind his back, his detractors referred to him as **His Rotundity**.

A Serious Student

John Adams was a graduate of Harvard. One of his first acts as President was to establish the library that became the **Library of Congress**. He signed the legislation in 1800 *"for the purchase of such books as may be necessary for the use of Congress."* The first 740 books and 30 maps were ordered from London publishers and were held in the unfinished Capitol. Today the Library of Congress is the **world's largest library** and contains a collection that fills some 650 miles of shelving in three buildings.

The White House Waiting Room

John Adams was elected our nation's first **Vice President**. It would appear that he did not care for the two terms he served under George Washington. It was frustrating to a man who had held active and exciting jobs. He wrote to his wife Abigail, *"My country has in its wisdom contrived for me the most insignificant office that ever the invention of man contrived or his imagination conceived."*

In the Heat of Battle

!*!

For sheer **slander**, few campaigns have compared to the heated runs between **Thomas Jefferson** and **John Adams**. The supporters of Adams said that Jefferson was a coward, a demagogue, a trickster, a **fraud**, a **lunatic** on the subject of France, and an atheist (causing some New Englanders to hide their Bibles so he could not confiscate them).

Not to be outdone, Jefferson supporters claimed that Adams planned to marry his son to one of the daughters of King George III. Adams himself wrote, *"If he (Jefferson) is elected, murder, robbery, rape, **adultery**, and **incest** will be openly taught and practiced!"* It makes you feel better about today's "attack ads," doesn't it!

!*!

Born: *Shadwell, Albermarle County VA, April 13, 1743*
Died: *Monticello VA, July 4, 1826*

The Sage of Monticello

Presidents on the Presidency

66 **Never did a prisoner released from his chains feel such relief as I shall on shaking off the shackles of power.** 99

— **Thomas Jefferson**

The First

On March 4, 1801, **Thomas Jefferson** walked the one block from Conrad's boardinghouse, where he was living, to the Capitol for his inauguration. His was the first presidential **inauguration** to take place in Washington, D. C.

The First Federal Bailout

"This ticket will entitle the holder thereof to such prize money as may be drawn to its numbers in the JEFFERSON LOTTERY."

In 1826, **Thomas Jefferson** was so deeply in debt that a public **lottery** was planned on his behalf. Fortunately, friends of Jefferson were able to raise the thousands of dollars needed to save the ex-President from bankruptcy.

His friends had already bailed Jefferson out once. In 1814, Jefferson offered his own personal library, over 6,000 volumes, to replace the Library of Congress, burned by British troops. Congress voted him about $24,000 for the books (a large sum in those days!).

As a practical joke, Jefferson had a number of books (which graphically described the decadence and corruption of monarchies) rebound with matching covers as if a multi-volume set, titled *The Book of Kings*. He knew Congressmen looking for support for monarchial institutions would have quite a shock, and Jefferson would have the last laugh!

Big Ideas

Everyone knows that Benjamin Franklin was a prolific inventor. Fewer people realize that **Thomas Jefferson** also had an **inventive** mind. Among his many **inventions** were a swivel chair, the lazy susan, a letter copying device, and an early pedometer!

Jefferson's chair

Big Ben

Benjamin Franklin served brilliantly as American ambassador to France. **Thomas Jefferson**, who followed Franklin was received by the French foreign minister, the Comte de Vergennes.

"You replace Dr. Franklin?" inquired the French count.

"No one can replace Franklin," replied Jefferson. *"I merely succeed him."*

Whole Lotta Shakin' Goin' On

Thomas Jefferson was the first to **shake hands** with visitors to the White House. Washington and Adams had merely bowed to their guests. Jefferson began the custom of shaking hands at a reception to mark the Fourth of July in 1801.

Hail to His Chef

At a time when a turkey cost 75¢ and a hog $3.00, **Thomas Jefferson** frequently spent as much as $50 a day on groceries. His White House **wine bill** alone was almost $11,000. Many of his gourmet delicacies were imported from Europe, and his chef came from France.

His dining table was round to discourage formality. It was a rather "**first-come, first-served**" boardinghouse arrangement, which Jefferson called "**pêle-mêle**." The person most upset by this congenial approach was protocol-minded British Ambassador Anthony Merry. Following one of Jefferson's dinner parties, Merry reported angrily that he had lost his seat to a Congressman who was faster.

23

Born: *Port Conway VA, March 16, 1751*
Died: *Montpelier VA, June 28, 1836*

Father of the Constitution

Presidents on the Presidency

66 The aim of every political constitution is, or ought to be, first to obtain for rulers men who possess most wisdom to discern, and most virtue to pursue, the common good of the society; and in the next place, to take the most effectual precautions for keeping them virtuous whilst they continue to hold their public trust. 99

—James Madison,
   Federalist Papers Number 57

Little Jemmy

James Madison was the smallest President. He weighed only **100 pounds**! When he walked with six-foot **Thomas Jefferson**, one observer said that they looked as if they were on their way to **"a father and son banquet."**

Third Term's the Charm?

President **James Madison** was elected to two full terms. He served two full terms. He had two different Vice Presidents. Both of them **died** before the end of the President's term. Good thing he didn't run for a third term. He might have had trouble finding a running mate.

Grr-rrr

He was the first President to wear **long trousers** (in fact, his successor, **James Monroe**, is known as "the last of the knee-breeches.") He also wore a jacket made from wool from his own sheep. However, Madison was a **Little Tiger**. He was the only President who actually participated in battle while in office. He directed a gun battery during the War of 1812.

long trousers

Politicians Spend Their Own Money

James Madison and **James Monroe** decided to become partners in a land speculation operation. Land in the **Mohawk Valley** of New York seemed a good investment. George Washington agreed, and the two friends bought 1,000 acres at $1.50 an acre.

Mohawk Valley

There was one small problem: the $700 down payment. Madison was **land poor**; he had no money. Monroe was a little better situated, so he took care of the down payment.

They could not repay the loan a year later, so they got their loan extended for three years, when Madison bought out Monroe. Madison finally sold the land—for a very small profit. As speculators, these Founding Fathers were a bust!

A BOXING MATCH, or Another Bloody Nose for JOHN BULL.

Bring It On!

One of **James Madison's** problems was his Secretary of War, John Armstrong. At a conference during the War of 1812, some of those present expressed the fear that the **British might attack** the city of Washington itself. Could the capital city be defended? The Secretary of War was astonished, *"Here? Here to this sheepwalk! Why the devil would they want to come here?"*

The City of Washington burning in 1812

Funny Founding Father

James Madison has a reputation for wisdom and foresight. What is less well known is that he was also a **delightful conversationalist** and a brilliant raconteur. In 1829, Madison attended a convention to update the Virginia state constitution. He proved to be in his element. One fellow delegate wrote that Madison's "*stock of racy anecdotes was the delight of every social board.*"

Born: *Westmoreland Co. VA, April 28, 1758*
Died: *New York City, July 4, 1831*

The Last of the Cocked Hats

The First

The first President to ride on a **steamship** was **James Monroe**. The ship was the *Savannah*, the first American steamship. In 1819, the *Savannah* became the first American steamship to cross the Atlantic.

Three on the Fourth

Of the first five Presidents, three died on the Fourth of July. In fact, two of them— **John Adams** and **Thomas Jefferson**—died only a few hours apart on the same day, **July 4, 1826**. Having been Jefferson's lifelong political adversary, Adams remained competitive until the end. His last words were, *"Thomas Jefferson still survives."* But unknown to Adams, Jefferson had died earlier that day. Five years later, on July 4, 1831, **James Monroe** died in New York City.

South Americans, Please Note...

James Monroe's seventh annual message to Congress, delivered on December 2, 1823, included reports on finances, military affairs, and generally routine matters. For those listeners who were still awake, the President made two references to American foreign policy, one early in the speech, the other near the close.

The two parts of the speech, put together, are the **Monroe Doctrine**. As it happened, the British Government approved of the same principles. For many years, it was the British Navy, not the Monroe Doctrine, which prevented seizure of South American lands.

Odd Coincidences

James Monroe was a member of a Congressional committee investigating charges of illegal speculation by Alexander Hamilton. The investigation established Hamilton's innocence, although Hamilton was having an **adulterous affair** with his accuser's wife. A few years later, political enemies of Hamilton published details of the whole sordid affair. Hamilton and Monroe were politically opposed, so Hamilton assumed Monroe was the source of the "**leak**." He challenged Monroe to a duel. In fact, Monroe was innocent, and the duel was called off – largely because of the efforts of Aaron Burr, Monroe's second and the man who, in 1804, was to kill Alexander Hamilton in a duel.

A Precedent for Presidents

James Monroe would have been the unanimous choice of the Electoral College in 1820. In fact, his second term is often called "**The Era of Good Feelings**." However, one delegate from New Hampshire felt a qualm. This delegate had no personal animosity to Monroe. In fact, he had voted for Monroe in the general election. However, he did feel that only George Washington should be a **unanimous** choice, so he voted against Monroe, with deep regret.

A CAPITAL Name!

Only one foreign country has a capital named for an American President. President **James Monroe** is the namesake of **Monrovia, Liberia**. The West African nation, was founded in 1822, Africa's first independent republic. It was established through efforts and contributions of the American Colonization Society, which had been established to free enslaved Africans and send them back as colonists. Monroe strongly supported the efforts of the Society, so the capital of Liberia was named in his honor. **James Monroe**, by the way, was, and continued to be, a slaveowner.

He Was Never "High Hat"

A cocked hat is the familiar **tricorne** hat worn by men during the American Revolutionary period. It went out of style after the French Revolution, along with powdered hair and knee breeches. In defiance of this "fashion revolution", **James Monroe** continued to wear his **cocked hat**, perhaps to show his conservatism or to remind people that he was the last link to the period of the American Revolution.

Born: *Braintree (now Quincy) MA, July 11, 1767*
Died: *Washington DC, February 23, 1848*

Old Man Eloquent

First Things First, Bitte!

In 1797, **John Quincy Adams** was appointed United States Minister to Prussia. It was a long and trying journey across a Europe in the throes of the early Napoleonic wars. Adams and his new bride arrived at the gates of **Berlin**. They were stopped by a young Prussian officer. Adams presented his credentials and explained that he was the new minister of the United States. The officer looked at Adams suspiciously, *"The United States? What are they?"* he asked.

His Day in Court

After leaving the White House, **John Quincy Adams** continued a life of public service. In 1841, a Spanish slave ship, the *Amistad*, had been **hijacked** by its unwilling African passengers and sailed into Long Island Sound. The US Navy towed the *Amistad* to New Haven, Connecticut, and imprisoned the Africans. A great legal imbroglio followed in which supporters of slavery demanded that the Africans be tried for piracy. Adams took the Africans' case and argued before the United States **Supreme Court**. One grateful African (a child) wrote to Adams that the Africans, *"…have got souls…..All we want is make us free."* "**Old Man Eloquent**" lived up to his name, and the Africans were granted their freedom.

the Amistad

The Bare Facts

John Quincy Adams was an inveterate **skinny-dipper**. Every day, weather permitting, he would rise, walk down to the Potomac River, hang his clothes on a tree, and take a swim *au naturel*. Perhaps the first female American reporter, Mrs. Anne Royall, wished to obtain an exclusive interview with President Adams. She simply followed the President to the river and sat on his clothes until he had answered all of her questions! History doesn't say, but can we assume it all went....**swimmingly**?

Famous Last Words...

Following his presidency, **John Quincy Adams** was elected to the House of Representatives from Massachusetts. The only ex-President to serve as a Representative, he was a member of the House from 1830 to 1848. The 80-year-old Adams was at his desk in the House when he suffered a **stroke**. He was taken to the Speaker's Office, where he died two days later, having regained consciousness only long enough to say, "*Thank the officers of the House. This is the last of earth. I am content.*"

Grandfather Knows Best

The grandson of **John Quincy Adams** recalled how he had decided not to go back to school when he was six or seven years old. He "*showed a certain tactical ability by refusing to start, and... He was in fair way to win, and was holding his own,... [when] the door of the President's library opened, and the old man slowly came out. Putting on his hat, he took the boy's hand without a word, and walked with him... up the road to the town... the boy reflected that an old gentleman close on eighty would never trouble himself... if a lad imbued with the passion of freedom could not find a corner to dodge around, somewhere before reaching the school door... But the old man did not stop, and the boy... found himself seated inside the school... Not till then did the President release his hand and depart.*"

29

Born: *Waxhaw SC, March 15, 1767*
Died: *Hermitage Plantation TN, June 8, 1845*

Old Hickory

Presidents on the Presidency

❝ **Dignified slavery.** ❞

— **Andrew Jackson**

The First

Andrew Jackson was the first President to ride on a **railroad train**, in 1833

Checking the Kitchen Cabinet

The President's official cabinet is selected with the advice and consent of the Senate. There have been instances, however, when a President wished for close advisers whom the Senators might perhaps have found less appealing. Many Presidents have had an "unofficial" cabinet. **Andrew Jackson** had such an unofficial, or **kitchen cabinet**, presumably because they were men who came in through the back door and were close to all the **goodies**.

An Ominous First

Richard Lawrence believed that **Andrew Jackson** was keeping him from his rightful position as **King of America**. He confronted Jackson in the Capitol in 1835 and fired two pistols. Both misfired. Lawrence was seized, adjudged insane, and committed to an asylum. It was America's first Presidential **assassination** attempt.

He Always Said Where He Was Going

Alfred was a retainer at **Andrew Jackson's** home, **The Hermitage**. When Jackson died, Alfred was asked if he thought that his master had gone to **heaven**. *"Well,"* answered Alfred, *"that's where he always said he was going, and if the General said he was gonna go there, that's where he went."*

Um...We'll Do Our Best, Sir!

The Battle of New Orleans was fought after the War of 1812 was officially over, but no one had told the two generals! His spectacular victory made **Andrew Jackson** a national hero and led the way to the White House. During the battle, Jackson saw that his gunners were firing over the heads of the advancing British troops. He called out to the gunners, *"Elevate them guns a little lower!"* They did—and to devastating effect!

Good Thing He Bought a Round-Trip Ticket

Andrew Jackson left the presidency with $90 in cash. His estate, The Hermitage, was thousands of dollars **in debt**. He was 70 years old and his retirement remained troubled financially until his death in 1845.

A Cheesy Party

There were no invitations for **Andrew Jackson's** first reception at the White House in 1829. Dress was informal, and guests were expected to amuse themselves. In an odd form of entertainment, Jackson's guests broke china, crystal, and windows, stood on damask chairs, tearing their elegant fabric with muddy boots, wrecked furniture, tore wall hangings, draperies, and each other's clothes. In the **melee**, there were fistfights, fainting spells, drunken brawls, and so much over-crowding that Jackson had to escape through a rear window, protected by a cordon of his friends. He spent his first night as President at a local hotel!

Apparently Jackson liked this kind of party. Shortly before he left office, the New York State dairymen presented the outgoing President with a 4-foot long, 2-foot thick cheese weighing **1,400** pounds. Jackson threw another party! The principal difference between the inaugural party and the farewell party was the smell. Uneaten cheese was ground into carpets and smeared on furniture, and it **reeked**...for weeks! Long after the party was over, the memory lingered on.

Born: *Kinderhook NY, December 5, 1782*
Died: *Kinderhook NY, July 24, 1862*

The Red Fox of Kinderhook

Presidents on the Presidency

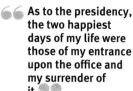

❝ As to the presidency, the two happiest days of my life were those of my entrance upon the office and my surrender of it. ❞

— Martin Van Buren

The First *American* President

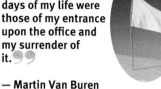

The first President born in the **United States** (after the American Revolution) was **Martin Van Buren**.

My Point Exactly!

They didn't call **Martin Van Buren** the "**Red Fox of Kinderhook**" and "**The Little Magician**" for nothing. A consummate politician, pleasant, smooth, personable, and deft, he was highly adept at the art of being non-committal. Nowhere were his skills better demonstrated than they were at Albany, New York, on July 10, 1827, before a group of woolen producers and manufacturers. The gentlemen in the audience were unanimously in favor of a high protective tariff on imported woolens. In the South, the feeling was equally strongly against the tariff. Van Buren's job was to keep both sides happy. The Fox spoke for an hour, and his speech was received with enthusiasm. When Van Buren had finished speaking, one wool buyer turned to a friend.

"*Mr. Knower, that was a very able speech.*"

"*Yes,*" agreed Knower, "*very able.*"

"*Mr. Knower, on which side of the tariff question was it?*"

The Albany Gang

Martin Van Buren, **Grover Cleveland**, **Theodore Roosevelt**, and **Franklin Roosevelt** served as Governors of New York before becoming President.

Getting Martin's O.K.

Martin Van Buren's nickname was Old Kinderhook, a reference to his hometown, Kinderhook, New York. **O.K.**, the abbreviation of his nickname, was used as a Van Buren political slogan. Many experts in that kind of thing believe this is how the term originated.

The Sun Also Rises

A Senator friendly to **Martin Van Buren** once bet that a fellow Senator could not get the notoriously noncommittal Van Buren to agree that the sun rose in the East. The betting Senator put the question to the President and eagerly awaited his reply, which was magisterially noncommittal, *"I invariably awake in the morning after sunrise, so I wouldn't know."*

An Unlikely Television Star

Martin Van Buren was dead a century before television was even invented, but he seems to be a favorite with **TV sitcoms**. An episode of *Seinfeld* featured a street gang who took Van Buren as their hero. And the television show *The Monkees* even featured the ex-President applying for dance lessons!

33

Born: *Berkeley Plantation VA, February 9, 1773*
Died: *Washington DC, April 4, 1841*

Old Tippecanoe

The First

The first President to have his **photograph** taken in office was **William Henry Harrison**, in 1841.

A Modern Dad in 1840

President **William Henry Harrison**, a market basket on his arm, did the family food shopping.

Up the Creek!

Tippecanoe is the name of a creek in northwest Indiana. In 1811, American forces led by **William Henry Harrison** fought a pitched battle with Indian troops led by the brother of **Tecumseh**, the great Indian leader. The American victory marked the end of Tecumseh's bid for power. (He died fighting for the British during the War of 1812.) Harrison became wildly popular as "Old Tippecanoe." When he ran for President, his supporters chanted **"Tippecanoe and Tyler, Too!"** (John Tyler was his running mate.)

Chief Tecumseh

Happy Father's Day, Mr. President

William Henry Harrison, married once, was the father of **ten children**—six boys and four girls. This is the record for children born to a single presidential marriage. His successor, **John Tyler**, was married twice. He had three sons and five daughters with his first wife, five sons and two daughters with his second. In siring fifteen children, Tyler was the most fatherly of all the Presidents.

Beginning a Presidential Tradition

Before the Whigs nominated **William Henry Harrison** for President in 1840, one of his supporters wrote, "*Say not one single word about his principles or his creed. Let him say nothing, promise nothing. Let no committee, no convention, no town meeting ever extract from him a single word about what he thinks now and will do hereafter. Let the use of pen and ink be wholly forbidden.*" That didn't leave Harrison's managers much to work with. Lucky for them, a Baltimore newspaper sneeringly wrote:: "*Give him a barrel of hard cider and a pension of $2,000 a year and he will sit the remainder of his days in a log cabin by the side of a 'sea coal' fire and study moral philosophy.*" Harrison's campaign managers seized on the quote and ran the "**log-cabin, hard-cider campaign!**" It was such a success that Americans fell in love with log cabin candidates. (In point of fact, Harrison had been born in a handsome, three-story brick plantation house in Virginia—a mere detail!)

A Lasting Campaign Slogan

Among the banners, buttons, and campaign materials of **William Henry Harrison's** cider and log cabin campaign of 1840, one item stood out, quite literally. It was a **ball**, a paper ball, perhaps six feet in diameter, inscribed with Whig political slogans. During the campaign, Harrison's followers enthusiastically pushed the huge ball from town to town, shouting what in effect became an additional slogan, "**Keep the ball rolling!**" As a party, the Whigs are gone, but their war cry lingers on!

Better a Man of Few Words

The shortest inauguration speech, only 133 words, was delivered by George Washington at his second inaugural on March 4, 1793. The longest, delivered by **William Henry Harrison** on March 4, 1841, contained 8,443 words and it **killed** him!

At a normal speaking rate, Washington's speech lasted about two minutes, Harrison's speech for an hour and ten minutes. The fact that the longest speech preceded the shortest presidential term was no coincidence. Harrison delivered his message outdoors, on the east portico of the Capitol. In spite of the cold and stormy day, Harrison refused to wear a hat or coat. Harrison caught a cold, the cold developed into **pneumonia**, and Harrison died a month later.

Born: *Greenway Plantation VA, March 29, 1790*
Died: *Richmond VA, January 18, 1862*

His Accidency

The First

The first **Vice President** to become President on the death of his predecessor, **John Tyler** was also the first President to marry while in office, in 1844. (The others were **Grover Cleveland**, in 1886, and **Woodrow Wilson**, in 1915.)

A Sudden President

John Tyler was surprised to learn that he was now President following the death of **William Henry Harrison**. He was literally surprised, on his knees, playing marbles with his sons! History does not tell us whether or not he finished the game before being sworn in.

What's in a Name?

John Tyler had many nicknames. Among them were **"Honest John"** because he was regarded as incorruptible. He was also called **"His Accidency"** since he had not been elected President. Tyler himself thought he was something of a political maverick.

In fact, he renamed his Virginia plantation Sherwood Forest, in honor of his Robin Hood role in politics. (Incidentally, this house, previously owned by **William Henry Harrison**, may be the only one in the United States owned by two different Presidents.) As an ex-President, Tyler went to the House of Representatives in 1861, but it was to the Confederate House of Representatives. He was the only President to serve in the Confederate Government.

Nevermore

Edgar Allen Poe once had an interview with President **John Tyler**. The interview was not a great success, sad to say. In fact, Poe arrived **roaring drunk** and didn't seem to have noticed that he was wearing his coat inside out.

Edgar Allen Poe

Horse Sense

John Tyler wrote the following epitaph for his **horse**:

"Here lies the body of my good horse, 'The General'. For twenty years he bore me around the circuit of my practice, and in all that time he never made a blunder. Would that his master could say the same."

Call the Cops!

John Tyler's nickname was "**The President Without a Party**" because he so alienated the Whig Party leaders that they disowned him! In fact, his entire cabinet resigned as a result of his policies and, as they left the White House after their protest resignations, they started a **riot** on the mansion's lawn!

A Gunshot Wedding?

John Tyler's first wife, Letitia, died while he was in the White House. Later, Dolley Madison arranged a boating party on board the *USS Princeton*, a new steamship. Among the other guests were New York Congressman David Gardiner and his very attractive daughter, **Julia**. During the cruise, it was decided to fire the massive guns of the new ship. One of the guns **exploded**, killing the Secretary of State, the Naval Secretary, and Congressman Gardiner. Julia was so overcome that she **fainted** into the widowed President's arms. They were married about a year later, after a secret engagement.

Whig Harmony

Born: *Mecklenburg Co. NC,
November 2, 1795*
Died: *Nashville TN, June 15, 1849*

Young Hickory

Having It Out Early

James K. Polk was not just a successful politician. He was also a man of great personal courage. At the age of 17, and at the hands of a backwoods Kentucky doctor, he submitted to a gallstone **operation**. (And this was long before anyone had heard of **anesthesia**!)

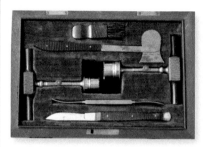

POLK No Fun at Him!

In the presidential campaign of 1844, the Whig Party crowed, "**Who the hell is James K. Polk?**" This ridicule reflected Democrat Polk's lack of charisma and fame. Nevertheless, he proved to be a hard-working and capable President. In fact, one historian has written that Polk was *"the one bright spot in the dull void between Jackson and Lincoln."* Polk was probably the only President to

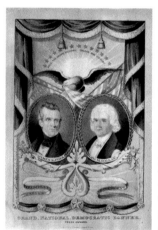

GRAND NATIONAL DEMOCRATIC BANNER.

draw up a list of objectives for his term and (even more surprising!) to accomplish all of them! Polk settled the border dispute between Canada and the Oregon Territory. He also successfully provoked the war with Mexico and won vast new territories for the United States. He wanted the borders of the United States to reach the Pacific— and he saw to it personally that they did.

The First Executive Secretary

James K. Polk had a long-time **intimate relationship** with his secretary. And his secretary was a married woman. But there was no "**White House scandal**." His secretary was also his wife, Sarah Childress Polk.

Coming from Nowhere

James Polk was not the first political "dark horse," nor the last. He is, however, famous for being plucked from obscurity as a compromise

candidate. At the time of his nomination, most people had never heard of him. Senator Tom Corwin of Ohio remarked upon hearing of the nomination, *"James K. Polk, of Tennessee? After that, who is safe?"* Incidentally, the term "dark horse" for an unlikely winner began as a racing term.

Chiefly Chosen...

Julia Tyler introduced the playing of "Hail to the Chief" to honor the President. Ironically, it was first used to greet her husband's successor, **James K. Polk**. The tune is an old Gaelic melody adapted by a British composer for use in a musical drama about Scotland, a musical version of Sir Walter Scott's

The Lady of the Lake, performed only briefly in 1811 without much comment. The tune lived on in the former colonies!

Oh, NOW I get it!

James Polk was astounded when former President Andrew Jackson attacked him for choosing James Buchanan as his Secretary of State. *"But you appointed him Minister to Russia yourself,"* the astonished Polk objected. Jackson admitted that he had, but he went on to explain that it was as far away as he could send Buchanan. He added that he would have preferred to send Buchanan to the **North Pole**, but the United States had no embassy there!

Mr. Ex-President

James K. Polk scarcely had time to enjoy his retirement from the presidency. In fact, he had the shortest retirement of any ex-President. **Worn out** from **overwork** during his single term in office, he lived for only three months, dying a mere 103 days after leaving office.

12 Zachary Taylor

Born: *Orange Co. VA, November 24, 1784*
Died: *Washington DC, July 9, 1850*

Old Rough and Ready

Tact

Zachary Taylor was serving as a general in the Mexican War when a young officer galloped up to the General's headquarters and announced that he had just seen **20,000 Mexicans** with 250 guns marching in the direction of the American forces.

"You saw **20,000 men**?" inquired the dubious Taylor.

"Yes, Sir." The enthusiastic young man replied.

"With **250 guns**?"

"Yes, yes."

"Well, then I must believe you," said the General, "but I would not have believed it if I had seen it myself."

Old "Who" and Old "What"

During the **Mexican** War **Zachary Taylor**, known as "**Old Rough and Ready**," and General Winfield Scott, known as "**Old Fuss and Feathers**," were on the same side— the American side. By the time the war was over, both had become national heroes. Then, the two generals opposed each other— each seeking the presidential nomination at the Whig Party convention. In this political battle, Old Rough and Ready defeated Old Fuss and Feathers. It sure has been a long time since candidates had names like that.

Well Connected

Zachary Taylor was related to quite a few famous Americans. Among others, he was a second cousin to **James Madison**, a fourth cousin to **Robert E. Lee**, and in a manner way too complicated to explain, he was also related to **Franklin D. Roosevelt**.

One Man, One Vote

Zachary Taylor voted only **once** in a presidential election, and he voted for himself.

Straight from the Horse's Tail...

Visitors to **Zachary Taylor's** White House were invited to keep a souvenir. They were told to collect a **hair** from the tail of **Whitey**, the horse Taylor had ridden during his splendidly successful Mexican War days. Whitey was easily found. He grazed on the White House lawn.

Ouch!
Hey watch it!

Marrying the Boss's Daughter

A young lieutenant had served on **Zachary Taylor's** staff during the Mexican War. He had been an outstanding soldier, but Taylor was less than enthusiastic about having the young man for a son-in-law. The general's daughter disagreed, and the lieutenant married Taylor's daughter Sarah. The young man went on to fame of a sort. He was **Jefferson Davis**, President of the Confederate States of America.

The Jury's Still Out...

On a hot July 4, 1850, President **Zachary Taylor** attended a corner-stone-laying ceremony for the Washington Monument. When the ceremony was over, Taylor returned to the White House, drank cold milk, ate cherries, got sick, and died on July 9. The exact cause of his death never has been determined. It was, possibly, the milk, the cherries, or the heat. More recently, one historian suggested that Taylor might have been **poisoned**. A Taylor descendant gave permission for an **autopsy** in 1991. Traces of the poison arsenic were found, but no more than would be found normally in a human body.

Sleeping on the Job!

March 4, 1849, happened to be a Sunday. **Zachary Taylor** refused to take office until Monday, March 5. His predecessor, John Tyler, had left office on March 3. So who was President of the United States on March 4? For one day, David Rice Atchison, the **President Pro Tempore of the Senate**, served as President of the United States, the shortest administration in US history. He said later that he was so tired from his Senate duties that he slept through most of his term!

z-z-z-z

Wise Words

> It is not strange....to mistake change for progress.
> — Millard Fillmore

The Last

Millard Fillmore was the last U.S. President to be neither a Republican nor a Democrat. His last words were allegedly, *"My only regret is that the Whig dies with me."*

Born: *Locke, NY, January 7, 1800*
Died: *Buffalo, NY, March 8, 1874*

The Wool Carder President

Now, Here's Your Homework

Abigail Powers was a teacher. One of her pupils was **Millard Fillmore**. Abigail taught Millard how to read and write. Millard married Abigail! Fillmore never forgot that he had come from humble beginnings. The British university, Oxford, offered Fillmore an **honorary degree**. Fillmore declined the honor because *"No man should accept a degree that he cannot read."*

Borrowed Splendor

Millard Fillmore had not been President long when he decided that his new position required a new carriage as well. He sent a White House servant to locate something suitable. The servant returned and announced with some triumph that he had found a **magnificent carriage**, which could be had cheap since the owner was leaving Washington and was anxious to sell the rig. The President thought the matter over carefully and then stated that he did not think a **second-hand** carriage was quite the thing for the President of the United States. The servant replied, *"Well, you are only a second-hand President, after all."*

Fillmore's Fictitious Bathtub

Bathtubs were something new and not quite safe in the 1850s. President **Millard Fillmore** went a long way toward cleaning America (and Americans) up when he installed the **first bathtub** in the White House. Great story! Unfortunately, also untrue! The whole "**bathtub hoax**" was invented by humorist **H.L Mencken** in 1917. Menchken later admitted he had never expected his harmless joke to be taken so seriously by historians.

H. L. Mencken

"I Know Nothing"

After leaving the White House, **Millard Fillmore** ran once again for the Presidency as the candidate of the Nativist or "**Know Nothing Party**." Since many of its activities were cloaked in secrecy, its members were instructed, when questioned about the party, to answer "*I know nothing.*" The name stuck. Since they were largely people who feared a papal takeover of the United States, they may have been telling the truth!

If You Can't Stand the Heat...

Clearly a man who wanted to be thoroughly up-to-date, **Millard Fillmore** purchased a cast-iron cooking stove for the White House kitchen. The stove worked, but the cook refused! Fillmore solved this "kitchen crisis" by going to the U.S. Patent Office, studying a model of the stove, and personally instructing the cook in the mysteries of its operation.

Opening Up

Millard Fillmore was determined to open xenophobic Japan to US trade. To that end he sent Commodore Matthew Perry to *Edo* (now Tokyo) harbor. The Japanese called Perry's steamships "**great, black dragons**." To sweeten the deal, Perry delivered lavish gifts, including a working steam locomotive with 350 feet of track, a lifeboat, a telescope, and a wide variety of firearms and liquor. The Japanese were reported to be delighted with their gifts, but they understood that they had no choice; they signed the treaty and Japan opened its ports to the world.

14 Franklin Pierce

Born: *Hillsboro NH, November 23, 1804*
Died: *Concord NH, October 8, 1869*

Handsome Frank

A Military Mind

Much was made of Franklin Pierce's lack of military experience when he became a general during the Mexican War. One political opponent swore that the following event actually happened. Pierce was ordered by his commander to make a "**feint**" in front of the enemy. Accordingly, Pierce rode his horse to the front of the lines, where he fell off and lay helplessly on the ground. When a more experienced soldier asked him what he was doing, Pierce replied testily, *"I am following orders. I am fainting!"* (This story is so good, you really want it to be true!)

An Old War Wound

Franklin Pierce served as a brigadier general in the **Mexican War**, but not for long. There he was, sitting on his horse at the start of his first battle. The horse didn't like the battle, the noise, or the artillery shells bursting all around. The horse panicked and bucked, throwing Franklin Pierce against the pommel of the saddle – hard!

Then to add injury to injury, the horse fell, landing on Pierce, and wrenching the newly minted General's knee. When he recovered from the shock of the first injury, Pierce discovered that he could not walk! Pierce was hospitalized and remained in Mexico only long enough to acquire a severe case of a local intestinal ailment known as "**Montezuma's Revenge**."

During the mud-slinging presidential campaign of 1852, the unkindest cut made by the opposition was that Franklin Pierce had not conducted himself heroically in the Mexican War at all.

Two Spirited Perspectives

Some historians say that **Franklin Pierce** was an **alcoholic**. Other historians say that Franklin Pierce was a reformed alcoholic. Which just goes to prove that some historians are kinder than other historians. Pierce certainly did not help his own legacy very much. After losing the Democratic renomination in 1856, he is said to have remarked, *"There's nothing left to do but get drunk."* This seems to have been a philosophy he took seriously. He once ran over an elderly woman while out for a ride. There were not **DUI** charges in those days, so we'll never know!

College Pals

Franklin Pierce was a graduate of Bowdoin College, Brunswick, Maine, Class of 1824. Among his schoolmates and friends at Bowdoin were **Henry Wadsworth Longfellow** and **Nathaniel Hawthorne**.

Still friends 40 years later, Pierce and Hawthorne went off on a vacation to the White Mountains. Hawthorne, author of such illustrious works as *The Scarlet Letter* and *The House of Seven Gables*, wrote a sad ending to the vacation by (as he might have put it himself) succumbing. However, even Hawthorne seems to have had his limits. Pierce was so unpopular by the time of the writer's death that the ex-President was not asked to be a **pallbearer** at Hawthorne's funeral.

Hawthorne

Longfellow

I Thin' I Can

Franklin Pierce was by no means the first choice of his party in 1852. He wasn't even an early choice. He was the walking definition of a "**dark horse**" candidate. While Nathaniel Hawthorne maintained that Pierce was "**deep, deep, deep**," others were less impressed. A local man from Pierce's hometown remarked that it was true Pierce had been successful as a state attorney, and he had been a decent judge. He admitted Pierce had been all right as a Congressman. But there he drew the line, As President, the local man opined, *"…when it comes to the whole United States, I do say that, in my judgement, Frank Pierce is agoin' to spread durned thin."*

45

Born: *Mercersburg PA, April 23, 1791*
Died: *Lancaster PA, June 1, 1868*

Old Buck

Presidents on the Presidency

> If you are as happy in entering the White House as I shall feel on returning to **Wheatland** *(Buchanan's home in Pennsylvania)* you are a happy man indeed.

— **James Buchanan to Abraham Lincoln, in 1861**

Have You Been Talking to Walt Whitman?

"**I like the noise of democracy.**"
—James Buchanan

Only One...

James Buchanan never married, so he is our only **bachelor** President. Buchanan was engaged at one time to Anne Coleman, whose father was one of America's first **millionaires**. Some unkind observers said that Buchanan was marrying Anne for her money. Anne decided to visit her sister in Philadelphia. There, and without warning, she died! The attending physician attributed her death to an attack of what he called "**convulsive hysteria**." *(This is the only recorded instance of this malady in medical history.)* For **James Buchanan**, a half-century of bachelorhood lay ahead. It was not entirely lonely, however. For years, Buchanan shared his living quarters with William Rufus King, America's only bachelor Vice President!

A Warm Reception

One of **James Buchanan's** White House guests was England's **Prince of Wales**. The future Edward VII slept in Buchanan's room while Buchanan spent the night on a sofa.

On another occasion there was a large delegation from **Japan**, the first such group ever sent abroad by that nation.

And then there was the young Indian brave who shouted a harangue to the effect that the White House belonged to the Indians, the ground it stood on belonged to the Indians, and that personally he was prepared to fight to get them back. The President, a man of considerable diplomatic experience, managed to calm his visitor with a few platitudes. Pity he was unable to do the same when Southern states started seceding in the final days of his Presidency.

The Prince of Wales

Ouch!

Historian Kenneth Stampp described **James Buchanan** as "*…the consummate 'doughface.' A northern man with southern principles.*" If you think that's bad, you should look into presidential ratings. These polls of professional historians, taken at regular intervals, consistently place Buchanan either **dead last** or next to last in the order of effective Preidents! But it was even worse when Buchanan was alive. Gossips referred to the Buchanan-William King pair as "**Miss Nancy**" and "**Aunt Fancy**." And you thought politicians were rough today!

Seeing It His Way

Photographs of **James Buchanan** show that he was a distinguished-looking man. He had a peculiar habit of tilting his head slightly to one side. Less charitable critics said it was the souvenir of a botched attempt to hang himself. Actually, Buchanan was **far-sighted** in one eye and **nearsighted** in the other, which probably helped him to see both sides of every question!

Born: *Hardin (now Larue) Co. KY, February 12, 1809*
Died: *Washington DC, April 15, 1865*

The Rail-Splitter

Presidents on the Presidency

❝ I'm like the man who was tarred and feathered and ridden out of town on a rail. When they asked him how he felt about it, he said that if it weren't for the honor of the thing, he would rather have walked. ❞

— Abraham Lincoln

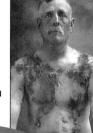

The First

The first President born outside the 13 original states was Abraham Lincoln.

DU PAGE COUNTY CENTENNIAL

LINCOLN ★ DOUGLAS ★ DEBATE

AUGUST · 27ᵀᴴ
WEST CHICAGO

He Who Laughs Last

The Lincoln-Douglas debates thrust **Abraham Lincoln** into national prominence. Somewhat obscured by the importance of the debates—their clarification of the **slavery** question—was a more local matter. The men were stating their respective positions in order to win a Senate seat from Illinois. Lincoln won national prominence, but Douglas won the Senate seat. The loss occasioned Lincoln to say that he felt like the boy who had **stubbed** his toe. It hurt too bad to laugh, and he was too big to cry.

Have Faith

Three Presidents, **Thomas Jefferson**, **Abraham Lincoln**, and **Andrew Johnson**, had no formal **religious** affiliation.

God Doesn't Mind

Mary Todd Lincoln came from a family so socially prominent that **Abe Lincoln** described it this way:

"God spells His name with one d but the Todds spell theirs with two."

Not Just Whistling Dixie

On April 10, 1865, Washington crowds, overjoyed at the news of **Robert E. Lee's surrender**, surged around the White House, cheering and calling for the President to come out and make a speech. **Abraham Lincoln** appeared, quieted the throng, and promised to make a few remarks. But first, he said, turning toward the members of a nearby band, he had a request. He would like the band to play "**Dixie**." Why "Dixie?" The crowd stirred restlessly. Was this another one of Lincoln's jokes? " 'Dixie,' " he said, "is one of the best tunes I have ever heard, and now we have captured it." The crowd cheered lustily as the band swung into "Dixie."

Times to Think Again

A number of contemporary newspapers reviewed Lincoln's **Gettysburg Address**. One of these was the *Chicago Times*. The Times had this to say:

> The cheeks of every American must tingle with shame as he reads the silly, flat and dish-watery utterances of the man who has been pointed out to intelligent foreigners as the President of the United States.

Upside Down

General Joseph **"Fighting Joe"** Hooker was one of many Union generals to precede Ulysses Grant. Hooker wished to give the impression of his busy approach to capturing the Confederate Army. He headed one dispatch **"Headquarters in the Saddle."** President **Abraham Lincoln** was unimpressed. *"The trouble with Hooker,"* he sighed, *"is that he has his headquarters where his hindquarters ought to be."*

A Small Favor

By late 1862, **Abraham Lincoln** was rather tired of waiting for General George McClellan to march against the Confederate army in Virginia. The **exasperated** President sent the general a brief message, *"If you don't want to use the army, I should like to borrow it for a while. Yours respectfully, A. Lincoln."*

Words of Wisdom

"Public discussion is helping to doom slavery," remarked Abraham Lincoln in 1860. *"What kills a skunk is the publicity it gives itself."*

Born: *Raleigh NC, December 29, 1808*
Died: *Carter Station TN, July 31, 1875*

Old Andy

Presidents on the Presidency

66 **I feel incompetent to perform duties ... which have been so unexpectedly thrown upon me.** 99

— **Andrew Johnson.**

Baked, But Still Not Warm

Secretary of State William H. Seward was the man primarily responsible for the purchase of Alaska from Russia for **$7,200,000**. Although this amounted to less than two cents an acre, a bargain at any time, perhaps the American people were more economy-minded than they are today. They considered the purchase an extravagant foolishness and referred to Alaska as "**Seward's Folly**." **Andrew Johnson** was President at the time and he, too, came in for his share of the "glory." Those who didn't call it "Seward's Folly" referred to Alaska as "**Andy Johnson's Polar Bear Garden**." The elegant Delmonico's restaurant in New York City named its new ice cream dessert "**Baked Alaska**." (Beginning in the late 1880s, a total of $250 million dollars worth of gold was later mined in "**Seward's Icebox**.")

Fathers of Their Country

Andrew Johnson was 19 when he became a father for the first time. John Tyler was 70 when he became a father for the last time. And there are still some people who call baseball the American Pastime!

White House Mice

Andrew Johnson found white mice in his bedroom in the White House. He fed the mice, but he never claimed them as pets!

Unimpeachable Friendship

Six years after he left Washington **under a cloud**, ex-President **Andrew Johnson** returned in triumph. The newly-elected Senator from Tennessee, the only ex-President to be elected to the Senate, Johnson entered the Senate Chamber to find his desk covered with **flowers**. He was greeted warmly by many of his associates, and by a cheering spectators' gallery. Senator Oliver P. Morton, however, turned away in embarrassment. Once a close friend of Johnson, he had voted for conviction during Johnson's **impeachment** trial. Johnson saw Morton and went over to him. The Senator from Tennessee extended his hand. The Senator from Indiana took it gladly.

Two Slave Presidents

Enslavement of blacks wasn't the only kind of slavery practiced in this country. The **indentured servant** was a different kind of slave, bound by a contract to work for a master who, in effect, owned him for the term of the contract. As boys, Presidents **Millard Fillmore** and **Andrew Johnson** were indentured servants. They didn't like it. Johnson, indentured to a tailor, ran away. The tailor took out an ad in the Raleigh, *North Carolina, Gazette*, offering a $10 reward for the return of the future President. There were no takers. Fillmore, indentured to **a clothmaker**, served his master for several years and finally bought his freedom for $30. Apparently Fillmore was worth $20 more than Andy Johnson.

Suiting Himself

Sometimes **clothes make the man**; sometimes it is just the opposite! Trained as a tailor by trade, President **Andrew Johnson** had all his clothes **custom-made** by President **Andrew Johnson**.

A Teacher's Reward

Eliza McCardle was a teacher. One of her pupils was Andrew Johnson. Eliza taught Andrew how to read and write. Andrew married Eliza.

Born: *Point Pleasant OH, April 27, 1822*
Died: *Mt. McGregor NY, July 23, 1885*

Hero of Appomatox

A Tin Ear

Ulysses S. Grant was apparently not a great musician. Said Grant, *"I only know two tunes. One of them is 'Yankee Doodle,' and the other one isn't.*

Guess Who?

❝ **Twice in my life I killed wild animals, and I have regretted both acts ever since.** ❞

— **Ulysses S. Grant**

Eyes on the Ball

A friend tried to persuade **Ulysses S. Grant** to take up golf as a good form of exercise. Grant consented to be an observer.

Arriving at the course, the first thing they saw was a tyro swinging his driver vigorously but missing the ball each time. *"That does look like very good exercise,"* agreed Grant. *"What is the little white ball for?"*

Ladies … AND a Gentleman

Ulysses Grant may have dressed sloppily, but there was nothing slovenly about his manners. Once a young officer at the mess table attempted to tell an off-color story. He introduced his topic with the sly remark, *"I see there are no ladies present."* To which Grant was heard to say, *"No, but there IS one gentleman!"*

What's In a Name?

When he arrived at **West Point**, he found that the representative who had appointed him had filled out the papers incorrectly. As a result, the rolls listed "Ulysses Simpson Grant" rather than his actual name "Hiram Ulysses Grant." The new plebe was happy to let the error stand. It tuned out well, since he was known during the Civil War as "**Unconditional Surrender**" Grant, using his Academy-acquired initials.

Is that you Hiram?

A Fast Track Politician

While President, **Ulysses S. Grant** drove his **buggy** through the streets of Washington. He was stopped by a policeman and fined twenty dollars for **speeding** on the capital's streets. To make matters worse, his buggy was confiscated, and he had to walk back to the White House!

A Legal Question

Before becoming President, Ulysses S. Grant was known for appearing shabby and poorly dressed. One stormy night he entered an inn where a number of local lawyers were clustered around a **blazing fire**. One lawyer said, *"Well, here is a stranger who looks like he rode through hell to get here.' How did you find things down there, stranger?"* *"Just like up here,"* Grant admitted. *"lawyers were closest to the fire."*

The Streets Are Flooded!

Following his term as President, **Ulysses S. Grant** and Mrs. Grant took a world tour. He was particularly impressed with **Venice**, but he did have one little suggestion. The city would be greatly improved if they **drained** it.

Getting the (West) Point

"Going to West Point," wrote Ulysses S. Grant in his Personal Memoirs, *"would give me the opportunity of visiting the two **great cities** of the continent, **New York** and **Philadelphia**. This was enough. When these places were visited I would have been glad to have had a steamboat or railroad collision, or any other accident happen, by which I might have received a temporary injury sufficient to make me ineligible, for a time, to enter the Academy. Nothing of the kind occurred, and I had to face the music...A military life held no charms for me, and I had not the faintest idea of staying in the army even if I should be graduated, which I did not expect."*

Born: *Delaware OH, October 4, 1822*
Died: *Fremont OH, January 17, 1893*

His Fraudulency

Presidents on the Presidency

66 **The President of the United States should strive to be always mindful of the fact that he serves his party best who serves his country best.** 99

— **Rutherford B. Hayes**

The First

The first President to visit the **West Coast** was **Rutherford B. Hayes**, who arrived in San Francisco, in September 1880.

Double Trouble

Rutherford B. Hayes won the hotly disputed 1876 election, but some believed that his opponent, Samuel Tilden, might try to stage a **coup** to seize the office. (Anyone who believed this did not know the highly ethical Tilden!) To prevent such a disaster, Hayes dined with outgoing President Ulysses Grant the night before the inauguration. During the meal, the **Chief Justice** of the Supreme Court slipped into the room and quietly administered the oath of office to Hayes. Thus, just once, and for less than 24 hours, the United States had **two Presidents**.

Zero Proof

Mrs. Rutherford B. Hayes was known as "**Lemonade Lucy,**" for she permitted no beverage stronger than that to be served at White House functions. A guest, describing one reception, remarked, *"The water flowed like wine."*

A Sincere Endorsement

"Uncle Birchard read John Ruskin. He was the favorite author with him. Not with me. Mine is and for forty years has been Emerson." **Rutherford B. Hayes** (guess where the B. came from!) was not exaggerating when he wrote this comment in 1891. In fact, he had actually met **Ralph Waldo Emerson** and was changed by the event. Throughout his life, Hayes returned again and again to the writings of "The Sage of Concord."

William A. Wheeler

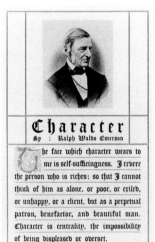

A Fair Question

Republican Party leaders were discussing who should run as **Vice-President** with candidate **Rutherford B. Hayes**. The name of William A. Wheeler was proposed to Hayes, who answered with a question that was admirable for its simplicity, its directness and its candor.

"I am ashamed to say, Who is Wheeler?" asked Hayes.

(Hayes might well have been ashamed. Wheeler was famous for his honesty. When Congress voted itself a pay increase in 1873, he voted against the bill and returned his salary increase to the Federal Treasury.)

The Son Also Rises

Two sons of Presidents have been awarded the **Congressional Medal of Honor**. **Rutherford B. Hayes'** son Webb received the medal for his actions on December 4, 1899, in the Philippine campaign of the Spanish-American War.

Theodore Roosevelt's son, Theodore Roosevelt, Jr., was awarded the medal for his performance as the only general to land in the first wave of troops at Normandy on June 6, 1944, D-Day.

Born: *Orange OH, November 19, 1831*
Died: *Elberon NJ, September 19, 1881*

The Canal Boy

An Embarrassment of Riches

Following the presidential election of 1880, **James A. Garfield** found himself in a **unique** position.

He had just been elected to the presidency. Earlier that year he had been elected by the Ohio legislature to serve as a United States Senator from that state, his term to begin the following March. President-elect, Senator-elect Garfield already had a job. He was, as he had been since 1862, an Ohio member of the U.S. House of Representatives.

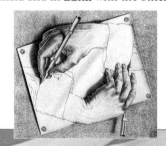

Presidential Resume

He was a **mule driver** and a **bargeman** on the Ohio and Erie Canal, (he fell overboard 14 times and he didn't know how to swim!) a professor of Latin and Greek, president of Hiram College (Ohio), an army general, a member of the House of Representatives, a Senate nominee, and President of the United States. **James Garfield** was a graduate of Williams.

Proof Positive

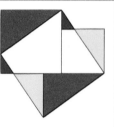

President **James Garfield** spoke seven languages, including Latin and ancient Greek. He also discovered a new proof of the **Pythagorean Theorem** while listening to a (probably dull!) debate in the House of Representatives. His proof, using a **trapezoid**, had never been applied before.

On the Other Hand...

President **James Garfield** had an astonishing **parlor trick**! A skilled linguist and, apparently, ambidextrous, Garfield was able to write simultaneously in **Greek** with one hand and in **Latin** with the other.

General-ly Speaking

The **eighteenth** President of the United States was **Ulysses S. Grant**. He was born in Ohio. He was a **general** in the Civil War.

The **nineteenth** President of the United States was **Rutherford B. Hayes**. He was born in Ohio. He was a **general** in the Civil War.

The **twentieth** President of the United States was **James A. Garfield**. He was born in Ohio. He was a **general** in the Civil War.

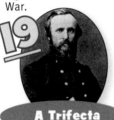

A Trifecta

Surrounded by Dangers

Until the latter part of the 1800s, there were many dangers to life in the nation's capital. Washington was sited on low, marshy ground. Muddy streets and stagnant canals, high humidity and penetrating dampness made summers in the capital a misery. On the other hand, malaria-carrying **mosquitoes** found Washington a splendid place to live. Most Presidents, especially those who wanted to survive their terms, left the city for the summer. In 1881, Mrs. James Garfield came down with **malaria**. While she recuperated at the family home at Elberon, New Jersey, the President decided to attend a college reunion. On July 2, as he walked through Union Station in Washington, the President was **shot**.

For Whom Bell Toils

President **James Garfield** probably would have recovered from his gunshot wounds had his doctors been less enthusiastic. It is almost certain that one of them caused a **streptococcus** infection when he inserted his **unwashed hands** into the President's wounds.

Alexander Graham Bell invented a special device for detecting the metal of the stray bullet inside the President's body. What Bell did not realize was that the iron **bedsprings** had not been removed from Garfield's hospital bed, which made his machine malfunction. The President died of infections from his wounds on September 19, 1881.

Born: *Fairfield VT, October 5, 1829*
Died: *New York City, November 18, 1886*

Prince Arthur

Presidents on the Presidency

66 **I may be President of the United States, but my private life is nobody's damn business!** 99

— **Chester Alan Arthur**

DO NOT DISTURB!

Gone, But Not Forgotten

Presidents **Andrew Jackson** and **Chester A. Arthur** had one thing in common: an **enduring love**. Both Presidents were widowers, both had adored their wives, and both followed a daily ritual of remembrance during their White House years. Jackson wore an ivory miniature of his late wife, Rachel, around his neck, removing it at night and placing it beside his bed so that it was the first thing he saw when he woke up. Arthur placed a **bouquet** of fresh flowers next to a photograph of his wife, Ellen, each day.

With Love

Justice for All

Chester Arthur inherited a hatred of slavery from his father. After passage of the **Fugitive Slave Act** in 1850, the young lawyer had eight recaptured Africans Americans freed before they could be sent back to the South. Arthur also represented an African American woman who had been refused a ride on a New York City streetcar. He won her case and got her a **$500 judgment**. (The decision also made discrimination on the city's transportation illegal.)

Where were YOU in 1955?

Rosa Parks

An Honest Guy

As a politician on the way up, **Chester Arthur** had been a part of the well-oiled influence machine of New York boss, Roscoe Conkling. Arthur was widely regarded as a **hack**, and a **disaster** for the country when he took over the White House. He astonished friends and foes alike by pushing hard for Civil Service reform, which would put an end to Federal patronage politics. As a result, the Federal bureaucracy became cleaner, more efficient, and most of all, less open to graft and corruption. No less a **cynic** than **Mark Twain** said, *"It would be hard indeed to better President Arthur's administration."*

Just in Time!

President **Chester Arthur** was instrumental in organizing the **time zones** of the world. In 1884, at his request, the International Meridian Conference was held in Washington, D.C. The conference established the meridian that ran through Greenwich, England, as the starting point, and established international standardized time zones that divided the earth. Railroad timetable and **long distance telephone users** have been grateful to Arthur ever since!

As the Twig is Bent...

A boyhood friend of the future President recalls **Chester A. Arthur** as a boyhood politician in Perry, New York: *"When Chester was a boy, you might see him in the village street after a shower, watching the boys building a mud dam across the rivulet in the roadway. Pretty soon, he would be ordering this one to bring stones, another sticks, and others sod and mud to finish the dam; and they would all do his bidding without question. But he took good care not to get any of the dirt on his hands."*

Retiring in Splendor

Chester A. Arthur surprised everyone by retiring from the White House in a glow of admiration and respect. In fact, widower Arthur received proposals from four young women the day he left office, a number which must stand as a record even today! He was known as "**Elegant Arthur**" throughout his life and was said to have had 80 pairs of pants in his wardrobe at its peak.

Born: *Caldwell NJ, March 18, 1837*
Died: *Princeton NJ, June 24, 1908*

Uncle Jumbo

Hey!
Hold On!
What
Happened
to
23?

One Heavyweight

Grover Cleveland, weighing in at about 260, was called, among other things, **Uncle Jumbo**. On one presidential campaign trip, Cleveland's train stopped at a small town. A grizzled old man made his way through the crowd, pushed up close to Cleveland, and stared at him. *"So you're the President,"* the man said to Cleveland. *"I am,"* Cleveland admitted genially. *"I've voted for a good many Presidents,"* said the man, *"but you're the first one I ever saw."* Cleveland smiled. *"Well, what do you think?"* The old man looked at Cleveland admiringly. *"You're a whopper,"* he said.

Burning With Righteousness

Grover Cleveland refused to stoop to scandal or **slander** in his campaigns, although both were common political practices of his time. During his first campaign for the White House, a nasty rumor surfaced about the marriage of his opponent, Republican James Blaine. A packet of papers, alleged to prove the charges, was offered to Cleveland. Cleveland bought the documents sight unseen. *"Are all the papers here?"* he demanded. When assured there were no more documents, he hurled the evidence into an open fireplace. *"The other side,"* he remarked, *"can have a monopoly of all the dirt in this campaign."*

Buffalo Gal

In Buffalo, New York, a **young widow** named Mrs. Maria Halpin had not one but a number of Prince Charmings, including a young bachelor named **Grover Cleveland**. When Mrs. Halpin was dutifully delivered of a boy, Cleveland took up the cost of supporting the boy, although there was some real doubt about who was the father. Shortly after the 1884 Presidential campaign began, a bit of **doggerel** was created:

> **Ma! Ma! Where's my pa?**
> **Gone to the White House.**
> **Ha! Ha! Ha!**

Keeping It Private

The election of 1884 matched Republican James G. Blaine against Democrat **Grover Cleveland**. Neither candidate had unsoiled political linen. Blaine, in his official position as Speaker of the House, had engaged in some highly **questionable** stock manipulation. Cleveland's reputation was sullied by an illicit **sexual exploit**, replete with offspring. This presented a **dilemma** to the voters, the solution to which was suggested, at the time, as follows: *"We are told that Mr. Blaine has been delinquent in office but blameless in private life, while Mr. Cleveland has been a model of official integrity but culpable in his personal relations. We should therefore elect Mr. Cleveland to the public office which he is so qualified to fill and remand Mr. Blaine to the private station which he is so admirably fitted to adorn."*

Okay, He Also Signed Some Laws!

Grover Cleveland's political enemies called him the "**Veto President**" for his habit of vetoing legislation he thought unwise or too expensive. In fact, during his two terms, Cleveland vetoed more legislation than the previous 21 Presidents combined! When Cleveland said, *"No!"* he meant "**No!**"

Oh, I Get it! Turn the Page for Benjamin Harrison, President 23!

Born: *North Bend OH, August 20, 1833*
Died: *Indianapolis IN, March 13, 1901*

Young Tippecanoe

Presidents on the Presidency

> 66 There has never been an hour since I left the White House that I have felt a wish to return to it. 99

— Benjamin Harrison

The Cold Shoulder

Benjamin Harrison gave rousing speeches which always brought his audiences to their feet, cheering wildly. In person, he was rather less effective. In fact, behind his back, he was known as "**the Human Iceberg**."

Garden Variety Pol?

Benjamin Harrison was proud of his family's service to the United States, but he more than once declared, *"I want it understood that I am the* **grandson of nobody***; I believe that every man should be judged on his own merits."* He was a terrific stump speaker, but personally, he appeared cold and distant. One politician said Harrison's handshake was "**like a wilted petunia**!"

Ain't Got No-Body!

The only man in the history of the United States to be the son of one President and the father of another was John Scott Harrison, son of **William Henry Harrison** and father of **Benjamin Harrison**. He, himself, was a two-term Congressman.

But things got really interesting after he **died**! John Scott died peacefully enough, at the age of 73, and was buried with dignity. Then—somehow—he went missing! A frantic search for the body determined that it was in the **dissecting room** of the Ohio Medical College. The body had not, of course, reached the college through the, shall we say regular, routes!

The result was the enactment of legislation that made the penalty for **bodynapping** very, very severe.

The New Addition

Benjamin Harrison's grandson was a week old when his proud grandpa wrote about the baby's progress in a letter to Cousin Mag. *"As to the baby,"* he wrote, *"I told his mother to say to him that if he would be patient until the snow is gone, we would all move out on the roof and give him the house."*

Lew-Dicrous

In 1888, an official campaign biography was written for **Benjamin Harrison** by a Hoosier neighbor. The neighbor was General Lou Wallace, already famous as the author of the celebrated novel "**Ben Hur**." One of Harrison's friends felt that the selection of Wallace as a biographer was a particularly good choice. As the gentleman put it, *"He did so well on 'Ben Hur' that we surely can trust Wallace with 'Ben Him'."*

First in Line

North and South Dakota had a serious rivalry about which state would enter the Union first. In 1889, President **Benjamin Harrison** was faced with a serious choice. Whichever bill he signed first would make the residents of the other state angry with him and with his party! Harrison had his Secretary of State **shuffle** the papers and obscure the names as he signed them. To this day, no one knows which of the **Dakotas** became a state first. It is traditional to list North Dakota first, but this is due to alphabetical order and not to any indiscretion from the Harrison White House.

Remember now, President 24 was also 22. Turn back to 60-61 to find him.

25 William McKinley

Born: *Niles OH, January 29, 1843*
Died: *Buffalo NY, September 14, 1901*

The Idol of Ohio

Presidents on the Presidency

❝ I have had enough of it, heaven knows! I have had all the honor there is in this place, and have had responsibilities enough to kill any man. ❞

— **William McKinley**

The First

The first President to campaign by **telephone** was **William McKinley**, in 1896.

He Needed God and a Globe

William McKinley pondered and prayed before signing the bill that declared war on Spain in 1898. He proudly told reporters, **"God** *told me to take the Philippines."* Unfortunately God had not supplied a map with this commandment. McKinley later admitted, *"I could not have told where those damned islands were within 2000 miles!"* Incidentally, Spain declared war first, so the United States **backdated** its declaration of war to three days earlier, so it could have the honor of starting the war!

Sweet William

First Lady Ida McKinley crocheted thousands and thousands of pairs of **bedroom slippers**, which she gave away. Childless, depressed, epileptic, she was treated by her husband with great tenderness. She sat by his side at public functions, and not infrequently, was seized by fits, at which point the President would place a handkerchief over her face until it had passed. The discomfiture of those present may well be imagined. *"President McKinley,"* said his friend and political mentor, Mark Hanna, *"has made it pretty hard for the rest of the husbands."* With the inner toughness of spirit that is sometimes surprising, Ida McKinley survived her husband's assassination for nearly six years. And it is not recorded that she suffered any seizures during these years either.

Presents on Other Presidents

66 **(McKinley) has no more backbone than a chocolate éclair!** 99

— Theodore Roosevelt

A Long Tax on Long Distance

William McKinley needed money to pay for the Spanish American War. Congress obligingly passed a tax on **long-distance telephone** service. It

was a popular tax since only wealthy Americans owned telephones in 1898. However, the tax was never repealed. Over a century later, in **2006**, the IRS announced that it would no longer collect the tax—presumably because the war's expenses had been paid off!

The Education President

President **William McKinley** was deeply mourned by the nation after his assassination. In addition to countless statues and other memorials, schools seem to have been a particular target for honoring the late President. There are McKinley **Elementary** Schools in Toledo, Marion, and Lakewood, OH, Fort Gratiot, Port Huron, and Sault Ste. Marie MI, Casper WY, Bakersfield and Redlands CA, Beaverton OR, Arlington VA, Montgomery County and York PA, and Parkersburg WV. There are McKinley **Middle** Schools in Baton Rouge LA and Cedar Rapids IA. And there are McKinley **High** Schools in Honolulu HI, Canton, Niles, and Sebring OH, Baton Rouge LA, St. Louis MO, and Washington DC.

Over His Dead Body!

Robert Lincoln was **Abraham Lincoln's** only surviving child. He rushed to his father's side on the night of Lincoln's assassination in 1865. In 1881, Secretary of War Robert Lincoln arrived at the Washington railroad station as **James Garfield** was shot. In 1901, Lincoln was not far from the Buffalo Exposition grounds when **William McKinley** was shot! Ironically, Robert Lincoln was once saved from death himself after he had fallen from a train platform . . . by Edwin Booth . . . the **brother** of John Wilkes Booth!

A Man OutSTANDING in His Field

An observation on President **William McKinley** by William Allen White:
"He was destined for a statue in the park and he was practicing the pose for it."

65

Born: *New York City, October 27, 1858*
Died: *Oyster Bay NY, January 6, 1919*

The Rough Rider

Presidents on the Presidency

66 I enjoy being President, and I like to do the work and have my hand on the lever 99.

— **Theodore Roosevelt**

The First

The first President to **leave the United States** during his term of office was **Theodore Roosevelt**, who went to Panama in November 1906 aboard the battleship *USS Louisiana* to inspect the progress being made on the Panama Canal.

For a moment, I thought you were important...

During his time as Vice President, **Theodore Roosevelt** happened to be staying at a hotel, which **caught fire**. All guests, Roosevelt included, were ordered to gather in the lobby. Roosevelt was tired of waiting, so he demanded to return to his room. *"Who are you?"* the fire chief demanded. *"I am the Vice President!"* Roosevelt snapped back. As he began to climb the stairs, the fire chief stopped him again, *"Wait a minute,"* he barked, *"Just what are you Vice President of?"* Roosevelt was aghast, **"Why I am the Vice President of the United States,"** he said. *"In that case, back to the lobby,"* the fire chief ordered. *"I thought you were the Vice President of this hotel!"*

High Praise

When **Teddy Roosevelt** visited the Hermitage, **Andrew Jackson's** home in Tennessee, he was offered a cup of coffee from the nearby **Maxwell House** Hotel. He drank the coffee enthusiastically and said, *"Good to the last drop!"* This statement became the motto of the Maxwell House coffee brand for the next 100 years.

Center-Staged

"Father always wanted to be the bride at every wedding and the corpse at every funeral," one of Theodore Roosevelt's sons remarked affectionately.

The Speech Did Have a Few Holes in It

In 1912, "**Bull Moose**" candidate, **Theodore Roosevelt** was in Milwaukee, Wisconsin, to make a speech. A Milwaukee resident named Shrank shot at the ex-President. His bullet passed through Roosevelt's eyeglass case and through the manuscript of the speech, which was folded in his pocket.

The **bullet** penetrated Roosevelt's chest but the thick manuscript slowed the velocity of the bullet. Being a gritty fellow, Roosevelt proceeded to deliver the speech. He began by saying, *"Friends, I shall ask you to be as quiet as possible. I don't know whether you fully understand that I have just been shot; but it takes more than that to kill a Bull Moose."*

The Rough Rider Rides Again...and Again... and Again

Theodore Roosevelt, was the **first** President to ride in an automobile (1902), submerge in a submarine (1905), and fly in an airplane (1910, as ex-President).

Teddy's Bear

The **teddy bear** was created and named in honor of President **Teddy Roosevelt**, who refused to shoot a bear cub while hunting. This inspired a political cartoon, which in turn triggered the manufacture of Teddy Bears in **Brooklyn**, NY.

Brought Back to Earth

Quentin Roosevelt was walking on stilts in a White House flower bed.

"Quentin, get out of there," called his father.

From his elevated position, son Quentin looked down at his father. *"I don't see what good it does **me**,"* grumbled Quentin, *"for **you** to be President."*

Local Pride

Theodore Roosevelt planned to hunt big game in Africa after he left the White House. Upon being told that **Theodore Roosevelt** had embarked on an **African safari**, financier and political enemy J. P. Morgan proposed the toast, *"Health to the **lions**!"*

Born: *Cincinnati OH, September 15, 1857*
Died: *Washington DC, March 8, 1930*

Big Bill

Presidents on the Presidency

66 **The nearer I get to the inauguration of my successor, the greater the relief I feel.** 99

— **William Howard Taft**

The First

The first President to have an automobile at the White House was **William Howard Taft,** in 1909. Actually he had four, a White Steamer, a Baker Electric, and two **Pierce Arrows**.

And They Were Friends!

In 1912, **Theodore Roosevelt** ran as a third-party candidate against his old friend and successor, Republican **William Howard Taft**. The race soon degenerated into **a verbal brawl** in which the two old friends virtually ignored the Democratic candidate (and eventual winner), **Woodrow Wilson**. Goaded to anger, Taft called Roosevelt a "**dangerous egotist,**" and "**a demagogue.**" TR was not one to mince words. He called Taft a "**fathead,**" a "**puzzlewit,**" and said he had *"brains less than a* **guinea pig.***"*

A Happy Court-ship

William Howard Taft was the only President also to serve as Chief Justice of the **Supreme Court**. Taft had never wanted to be President. The only position that he'd ever **really** wanted was to be Chief Justice. On June 30, 1921, eight years after his term as President was over, Taft was appointed Chief Justice by President **Warren Harding**. For over a century, the Supreme Court had met in whatever space was not currently used by Congress in the US Capitol. Taft argued successfully that the Supreme Court should have its own building! He served on the court until his death in 1930. He commented happily, *"In my present life I don't remember that I ever was President."*

Our Biggest President

William Howard Taft once found himself hope-lessly wedged into his White House bathtub. He had to summon help to be pulled out! A new, larger tub was ordered and installed. It was big enough to hold four ordinary sized Americans!

Cruelty to Animals

William Howard Taft weighed over **300 pounds**. Despite exercise, dieting, and outdoor activity, his weight never dropped below this figure. Prior to his election as President, he was Governor General of the Philippines. Secretary of War Elihu Root sent the governor a cable asking about his health. Taft cabled back that he was much better, and that he had just returned from a 25-mile horseback ride. Root promptly fired off this cable: "How is the **horse**?"

I'll Need a More Generous Offer

William Howard Taft was offered a Chair of Law at Yale. He declined it with a twinkle, saying that "a Sofa of Law" was more in keeping with his proportions

The First

The first President to open the **baseball** season was **William Howard Taft**, who threw out the first ball prior to the game between Washington and the Philadelphia Athletics at the start of the 1910 season.

Born: *Staunton VA, December 28, 1856*
Died: *Washington DC, February 3, 1924*

The Phrase-Maker

The First

The first President to cross the Atlantic while in office was **Woodrow Wilson**. He sailed in December 1918, aboard the *SS George Washington*, (a nationalized former German liner) to the peace negotiations that would formally end **World War One**.

Pithy From Woody

Woodrow Wilson said it.

66 Conservatism is the policy of 'make no change and consult your grandmother when in doubt.' 99

"I Am Dying for that Appointment!"

Before he became President, **Woodrow Wilson** was Governor of New Jersey. In 1911, he was shocked to learn that his friend, and one of New Jersey's senators, had **died** suddenly. While still absorbing his personal and political loss, Wilson received a phone call from a ruthlessly ambitious New Jersey politician. The man said he was anxious to take the late senator's place. *"That's all right with me,"* Wilson responded somberly, *"If the **undertaker** has no objections."*

Only One . . .

Only one President had a PhD. **Woodrow Wilson** received his **doctorate** from Johns Hopkins University in 1886. The subject of his doctoral thesis was *"Congressional Government, a Study in American Politics."*

He did additional on-the-job- research on this subject later.

That Was Quick

The 1916 presidential election was extremely close. It became clear that the election would be decided by a single state: **California**. Early California returns indicated that Republican **Charles Evans Hughes** was winning. The trend continued into the evening, and Hughes retired to bed confident that he had won. Then the voting tide changed. Wilson carried California, and won the election. The next morning, a reporter tried to reach Hughes for comment. An officious Hughes aide informed the reporter haughtily, *"The **PRESIDENT** is sleeping!"* The reporter was unimpressed, *"When he wakes up, give him this message. Tell him he's no longer President."*

He Made His Point

Woodrow Wilson had a program for ending World War I that included his famous "**14 Points**." Georges Clemenceau, French premier, was of the opinion that the United States was the only country in the history of the world that had gone from barbarism to decline without the intervening step of civilization. He took an equally dim view of the 14 Points. *"God Almighty gave us* **Ten Commandments**," said Clemenceau, *"and we broke those. Now we have Wilson who gives us Fourteen."*

Nobel Prizes

The Nobel Peace Prize was awarded to two Presidents. In 1906 it was awarded to **Theodore Roosevelt** for his work in ending the Russo-Japanese War. In 1919, it went to **Woodrow Wilson** for his efforts in creating the **League of Nations**.

Prayer Listing

Woodrow Wilson had suffered a **stroke**. His unsuccessful efforts to win the support of the Senate and the American people for his peace treaty had sapped his strength and led to a physical collapse. A delegation of Senators visited the sick President. *"We've all been praying for you,"* one of them said. Wilson's mind had not been affected by the stroke, nor had his sense of humor. *"Which way, Senator?"* he asked.

Born: *Blooming Grove OH,*
November 2, 1865
Died: *San Francisco CA, August 2, 1923*

President Hardly

Presidents on the Presidency

❝ **I am not fit for this office and never should have been here.** ❞

— **Warren Harding**

The First

The first President to ride to his **inauguration** in an automobile was **Warren Harding**, in 1921.

For Openers

Upon being informed that his party had **nominated** him for the highest office in the land, **Warren Harding** offered this statesmanlike utterance: *"We drew to a pair of deuces and filled."*

With Friends Like These...

Warren Harding was a man who trusted the friends he'd appointed to key positions in his administration. He shouldn't have, and he knew it, but only after the lid was off their **Teapot Dome scandal** and the corruption had boiled over. *"In this job I'm not worried about my enemies,"* said the disillusioned Harding. *"It's my friends, **my Goddamn friends**, who are keeping me awake nights."*

Harding's inauguration

He Bloviated Publicly

Warren Harding had the ability to **bloviate** whenever he wanted to. He was a master at bloviating. He should have been, for he popularized the term. Bloviating is the art of speaking, at great length and with great eloquence, and saying nothing…praising all the good things, damning all the bad things, and revealing one's own position on not a single issue.

But the Joke Was on Him

Warren Harding invited the popular comedian **Will Rogers** to visit him at the White house. Rogers offered to cheer the President up with some humor. *"Mr. President, I'd like to tell you all of the latest jokes."* Harding remarked philosophically, *"You don't have to. I have already appointed them to office."*

the Office-holders

Critical Reviews

Warren Harding was a popular speaker, especially when he **bloviated.** But everyone was not impressed. William McAdoo, **Woodrow Wilson's** Treasury Secretary, said of Harding, *"He spoke in a big bow-wow style of oratory. His speeches left the impression of an army of pompous phrases moving over the landscape in search of an idea…"* Another critic said his speeches were *"…rumble and bumble, flap and doodle, balder and dash…"* Poet e.e. cummings said that Harding was the only person *"…who ever wrote a simple declarative sentence with seven grammatical errors…"*

bow-wow

And Another First

The first presidential **radio** broadcast was made by **Warren Harding** in June of 1922. He spoke at the dedication of the Francis Scott Key Memorial at Fort McHenry, Baltimore, Maryland.

73

Born: *Plymouth Notch VT, July 4, 1872*
Died: *Northampton MA, January 5, 1933*

Silent Cal

Presidents on the Presidency

66 **I think the American public wants a solemn ass as President, and I think I'll go along with them.** 99

— **Calvin Coolidge**

Yankee Doodle Dandy

Calvin Coolidge was the only President to be born on the **Fourth of July**. The year was 1872.

There's Something Funny About Coolidge!

Few people today realize that **Calvin Coolidge** was one of our wittiest Presidents. So funny was he, in fact, that his Amherst College classmates voted him the **most humorous member** of the Class of 1895. Furthermore, they chose him to deliver the Grove Oration, a humorous speech given the day before graduation. Coolidge's utterly **deadpan** style of delivery was a side splitter and one he continued to use while President.

HA HA

Deep Thoughts on the Economy

Calvin Coolidge said it. *"When more and more people are thrown out of work, unemployment results."*

Trade Secret

Calvin Coolidge gave the following **advice** for handling White House visitors to incoming President **Herbert Hoover**. *"If you keep dead still,"* he said, *"they will run down in three or four minutes. If you even cough or smile, they will start up all over again."*

Presidents on Other Presidents

Calvin Coolidge was noticeably underwhelmed by **Herbert Hoover**. While he was supportive in public of the man who would succeed him, Coolidge was a great deal more candid in private. He once remarked, *"For six years that man has been giving me unsolicited advice – all of it bad!"*

Art Appreciation

One of the most striking and admired **portraits** in the White House is that of **Calvin Coolidge's** wife, **Grace Goodhue Coolidge**. The artist, Howard Chandler Christie, painted Mrs. Coolidge in a vibrant red dress beside her white collie, Rob Roy. President Coolidge didn't care for the dress or the painting. He stated firmly that he would have preferred her in white. Someone mentioned that the white dress and the white dog would not present sufficient visual contrast. The President was convinced and added that he supposed it was **cheaper** to buy a red dress than to dye the dog.

A Sinful Sermon

Grace Coolidge:
I'm sorry I missed the sermon. What was it about?

Calvin Coolidge:
Sin.

Grace Coolidge:
What did the minister say about it?

Calvin Coolidge:
He was against it.

Conversational Conservationist

Calvin Coolidge did not like waste —not even a waste of words. *"I do not choose to run for President in 1928,"* said Calvin Coolidge, a statement that has been remembered ever since for both its **brevity** and its **wisdom**. A White House visitor once gushed to the President, *"I bet someone that I could get more than two words out of you."* Coolidge smiled grimly, **"You lose."**

Born: *West Branch IA, August 10, 1874*
Died: *New York City, October 20, 1964*

The Great Engineer

Presidents on the Presidency

“ A few hair shirts are part of the wardrobe of every man. The President differs from other men in that he has a more extensive wardrobe. ”

— Herbert Hoover

The First

Herbert Hoover was the first President **born west** of the Mississippi River.

There Was a Lot of Firing That Year

Herbert Hoover was an extremely successful **mining engineer**, and his profession took him to many out-of-the-way places. In 1900, while working for the Chinese Bureau of Mines in **Tientsen**, he was caught in the **Boxer Rebellion**. For weeks the city was under siege. Finally Hoover felt that it had been strongly suggested "by way of **artillery**" that his services were no longer required.

Ours for a Song

The United States used a wide variety of **patriotic songs** at its formal national events. Contenders included *Hail, Columbia*, and *Yankee Doodle*. The US Navy selected the *Star Spangled Banner* in 1889 as the anthem it would use on official occasions. (And why not – the song commemorates a famous defeat for the British Navy!) It was made the official **national anthem** in 1931 when **Herbert Hoover** signed the Congressional resolution marking that choice.

I Got You, Babe!

The Great Depression affected everyone, even sports legends. **Babe Ruth**, the famous **Yankees player**, was asked by the management to take a pay cut. He refused to give back a penny. He was told that his salary was higher than that of President **Herbert Hoover**. *"Yeah,"* said the Babe. *"But I've had a **better year**!"*

Moo-ving Right Along

Herbert Hoover was disgusted when his efforts to promote economic recovery met with so little popular support during the Great Depression. He took the **criticisms** personally and complained to his predecessor Calvin Coolidge, who said soothingly, *"You can't expect to see calves running in the fields the day after you put the bull to the cows."* *"No,"* Hoover sourly agreed. *"But I would expect to see some contented cows!"*

I WILL DESTROY YOU CARTOONS And The Talent Show Present

introducing MELVIN McBEAN in

"BROTHER, CAN YOU SPARE A JOB?"

by TOM NEELY & GREG SAUNDERS

Lost in Those Zeroes

Some time after he left office and the **national debt** had more than doubled, **Herbert Hoover** commented on that poor creature, the **decimal point**, *"wandering around among the regimented ciphers trying to find some of the old places it used to know."*

Mr. Ex-President

Herbert Hoover, who left office under a cloud of criticism during the Great Depression, lived long enough to become revered as an **elder statesman** and **political sage**. He had been an ex-President for the longest time, 31 years, when he died in 1964.

Born: *Hyde Park NY, January 30, 1882*
Died: *Warm Springs GA, April 12, 1945*

FDR

The First

Franklin Roosevelt was the first Chief Executive whose **mother** could, and presumably did, vote for her son for President.

Never the Twain Shall Meet

In the 20th century, it became the fashion for an administration to have a label. There was **Teddy Roosevelt's** "Square Deal," **Harry Truman's** "Fair Deal," **Woodrow Wilson's** "New Freedom," and **John Kennedy's** "New Frontier." However, the best known of these, and the most enduring, was **Franklin Roosevelt's "New Deal."** The phrase was not actually Roosevelt's, although he did use it in his nomination speech. It came from an American source: Mark Twain's *A Connecticut Yankee in King Arthur's Court*.

And I Am Never Wrong...

In 1920, **Henry Cabot Lodge, Sr.,** the powerful and patrician Republican Senator from Massachusetts, offered his opinion of Franklin D. Roosevelt, at that time a young but up-and-coming Democrat. Said Lodge of Roosevelt, *"He is a well-meaning, nice young fellow, but light."*

Because

Thomas E. Dewey ran for President against **Franklin D. Roosevelt** in 1944 and lost. He ran again in 1948, against **Harry Truman**, and lost. Alice Longworth, Teddy Roosevelt's daughter and a kind of Washington monument in her own right, commented on Dewey's lack of popular appeal. *"How can you vote for a man,"* she asked, *"who looks like the bridegroom on a wedding cake?"*

Family Tradition

Franklin Roosevelt attended a dinner for White House correspondents in the spring of 1945. He had just been elected to his fourth term as President. Master of Ceremonies **Bob Hope** drew a loud laugh from his audience, especially from FDR, when he said, *"I've always voted for Franklin Roosevelt for President. My father before me always voted for Franklin Roosevelt for President."*

The Most Consecutive Executive

The 22nd Amendment to the Constitution provided that *"no person shall be elected to the office of President more than twice."* This amendment assures the record of **Franklin D. Roosevelt**, who succeeded himself, and succeeded himself, and succeeded himself. From March 4, 1933, until he died in office on April 12, 1945, FDR served a total of 4,422 days as President.

Shhh! Someone's Listening!

President **Franklin D. Roosevelt** hated the small talk required at official White House functions. He maintained that no one listened to a word anyone else said. To prove his point, he would occasionally tell a White House visitor, *"I **murdered my grandmother** this morning."* To his delight, no one even batted an eye, they simply murmured a few polite words and moved on. Once, however, to his dismay, he found a sympathetic listener. Having made his usual facetious declaration, Roosevelt was astonished to hear his guest say, *"Well, I am sure she **had it coming** to her."*

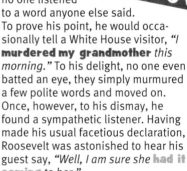

Frances the First

Frances Perkins was the first **woman** cabinet officer. She was appointed Secretary of Labor by **Franklin Roosevelt** in 1933. She held the post until 1945. When asked if being a woman was a **handicap**, she replied, *"Only in climbing trees."*

33 Harry S Truman

Born: *Lamar MO, May 8, 1884*
Died: *Kansas City MO, December 26, 1972*

Give 'Em Hell Harry

Presidents on the Presidency

66 **The White House is the finest prison in the world.** 99

Truman on Economics

Harry S Truman famously said that he was looking for an economic advisor who was **one-handed**. Why? Because as soon as his economic advisors finished telling him what to do, they would always say, *"On the other hand…."*

Just for the Hell of It

VOICE IN THE CROWD:
Give 'em hell, Harry!

HARRY TRUMAN:
I never gave 'em hell. I just told the truth and they thought it was hell.

Letting It All Out

One wonders how it feels to be relieved of the awesome responsibilities of the presidency. What had ex-President **Harry S Truman** done on his first day home again in Independence?

A question like that deserves an answer like that, and Harry provided it:

*"I took the **suitcases** up to the attic."*

He Looks Better From a Distance

Harry S Truman's stature has grown greatly since the days of his presidency. During the Truman administration, the feeling of many was expressed by Martha, the wife of Senator Robert Taft, who said of the President, "**To err is Truman.**"

A REAL Democrat

"I really admired and respected President Truman...Even when a Doorman or Butler was present, President Truman would introduce us to whomever happened to be in the room. If it was a King or Prime Minister, he still introduced us. He is the only President I worked for, or heard of, that did this..."

Carl Foreman

White House Doorman (1939-1956)

"The President [Harry S Truman] believed that nobody should have to wash someone else's socks or **underwear**, and he washed his own. I knew him for nearly eight years at the White House and Blair House. With all those problems he had...he still washed his own socks and underwear."

Lillian Rogers Parks

White House Seamstress (1931-1961)

Them's Fightin' Words!

A musical performance by Miss Margaret Truman was reviewed by a Mr. Paul Hume in the Washington Post. He rather uncharitably observed, *"She is flat a good deal of the time . . . cannot sing with anything approaching professional finish . . . communicates almost nothing of the music."* Upon reading the review, President Truman wrote his reply, *"I have just read your lousy review buried in the back pages. You sound like a frustrated old man who never made a success, an* **eight-ulcer man** *on a four-ulcer job and all four ulcers working. I never met you, but if I do you'll need a new nose and a supporter below."*

S for "Safer That Way"

Harry S Truman's paternal grandfather was Anderson Shippe Truman. His mother's father was Solomon Young. In an attempt to remain dynastically neutral, Truman's parents named him **Harry S Truman**. In fact, Truman had no middle name.

The First

The first President to broadcast from the White House over television was Harry S Truman, in 1947.

Born: *Denison TX, October 14, 1890*
Died: *Washington DC, March 28, 1969*

Ike

A Star Is Born

Asked if he knew **General Douglas MacArthur**, Dwight Eisenhower replied, *"Yes, I know him well. Very well indeed. I studied dramatics under him for years."*

Camping Out

Names were something of an obsession with the Eisenhowers. The Presidential retreat built by **Franklin Roosevelt's** CCC workers had been named "**Shangri-La**" after the setting of the James Hilton novel *Lost Horizon*. Eisenhower was more down-to-earth. He renamed the retreat **Camp David** after his grandson.

Never Look Back

An old friend from childhood days paid a call on **Dwight Eisenhower** at the White House.

Conversation turned to reminiscence and his friend remembered that Eisenhower's boyhood dream had been to become a famous baseball star.

"And you," said Eisenhower, *"wanted to be President of the United States."*

His friend nodded. *"That's right."*

"Well," said Ike, *"it looks like neither of us got his wish."*

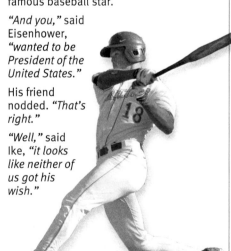

And What's Your Name, Little Boy?

A White House visitor asked **Dwight Eisenhower's** young grandson, David, what his name was.

"Dwight David Eisenhower," the boy replied. The President was seated nearby. *"If you are Dwight David Eisenhower,"* said the visitor, gesturing toward the President, *"then who is he?"* David answered without hesitation. *"That's Ike,"* he said.

Par for the Presidential Course

On February 6, 1968, while playing golf at Palm Springs, California, **Dwight D. Eisenhower** scored a **hole-in-one**. When asked, after leaving the White House, if retirement had affected his golf game, Eisenhower replied, *"Yep, a lot more people beat me now!"*

Tone Deaf

Before retiring to Gettysburg, General and then President **Dwight Eisenhower** hadn't dialed his own phone calls in years. A Secret Service agent watched as the ex-president picked up the phone and heard his first dial tone. Eisenhower looked puzzled, replaced the receiver, and tried turning the dial as if it were the combination on a safe. Finally, he turned to the bemused agent and asked for help. Once instructed, he spent the next hour happily dialing up his many friends for a post-presidency chat.

That's a Tough One

During the 1960 election, outgoing President **Dwight Eisenhower** gave his own Vice President and the next Republican candidate a rather **luke-warm endorsement**. At the end of a nationally televised press conference, Eisenhower was asked to list any **policy idea** that Richard Nixon had suggested and Eisenhower had adopted. Eisenhower's refreshingly honest response did not help Nixon's chances *"If you give me a week, I might think of one,"* he said. A delighted **John F. Kennedy** used the quote to great advantage in his winning campaign.

Tricky Dick

Ike

Flying High . . .

Dwight Eisenhower and **George W. Bush** are the only presidents to have **pilot's licenses**.

Born: *Brookline MA, May 29, 1917*
Died: *Dallas TX, November 22, 1963*

JFK

The First

John F. Kennedy was the first, and so far the only, **Roman Catholic** President of the United States.

Awesome Responsibility

66 Do you realize the responsibility I carry? I'm the only person standing between Richard Nixon and the **White House**! 99

— John Kennedy

Anchors Aweigh.....Finally!!!

For 172 years, the presidency was occupied either by men who had served in the Army or men who had seen no military service at all. There was not a **Navy** man among them. But, in 1960 all that changed and then it was **full speed ahead**: John Kennedy—Navy, **Lyndon Johnson**—Navy, **Richard Nixon**—Navy, **Gerald Ford**—Navy, **James Carter**—Navy. Five in a row for the Navy!

A Warm Reception

John Kennedy was on the campaign trail. He stepped before a rural audience, which had gathered to hear him speak. The audience applauded enthusiastically, and Kennedy expressed his appreciation. *"As the cow said to the farmer,"* he smiled, *"Thanks for a warm hand on a cold morning."*

One Size Fits All

On May 29, 1938, his 21st birthday, **John F. Kennedy** received a very nice birthday gift from his father: a **$1,000,000** trust fund.

Think About THAT!

Kennedy **children** are brought up to win political elections. Two of Bobby's were in a department store one day. The girl was behaving like a lady, but her younger brother was behaving like a little boy in a department store, and people were turning to look. She spoke to him sharply. *"Do be quiet. You're losing votes acting like this!"*

Money Talks

Shortly after he became President, **John Kennedy** publicly thanked **Clark Clifford**, the Washington

lawyer who had helped to effect a smooth transition between the outgoing Eisenhower administration and Kennedy's. At a dinner party, he said of Clifford, *"Clark helped us a great deal and asked for only one small favor in return . . . that we advertise his law firm on the back of one-dollar bills."*

Only One

Only one President was awarded a **Pulitzer Prize**. Author of *Profiles in Courage*, **John F. Kennedy** received the prize for biography.

Within the Family

When Father spoke, everyone in the Kennedy family listened, even if one happened to be the newly elected **President of the United States**. The day was pleasant, and Joe Kennedy decided it would be nice if they all went sailing. Jack didn't feel like going and said so. This simply wasn't done. They all looked at Jack. Then they all looked at Father. Joseph Kennedy was silent for a moment. Then he said, *"I don't think the President should have to go if he doesn't want to."*

Is That Good?

66 Washington is a city of **Southern** efficiency and **Northern** charm. 99

— John Kennedy

Born: *Stonewall TX, August 27, 1908*
Died: *San Antonio TX, January 22, 1973*

L.B.J.

Presidents on the Presidency

66 **A President's hardest task is not to do what is right but to know what is right.** 99

— **Lyndon Johnson**

The First

Lyndon Johnson nominated Civil Rights attorney, Thurgood Marshall, to the Supreme Court. Marshall was the first **African American** to hold a Supreme Court seat.

Thanks, Ma!

A very long time before **Lyndon Johnson** became President, he was a **bootblack**. During this period, his father bought a local newspaper. While her husband was away on a business trip, Lyndon's mother was in charge of the newspaper. The boy asked her if he could take an **ad** in the newspaper to promote his bootblack business. She agreed, and it was done. When Father found out about the ad he didn't say much, except, *"I bought a newspaper for my wife to advertise that my son is a bootblack."*

A Successful Marriage

Princess Margaret of Great Britain and her husband, **Lord Snowden**, were visiting the White House. President **Lyndon Johnson** took the occasion to give the Earl a piece of **husbandly advice**. *"I've learned that there are only two things necessary to keep your wife happy,"* said Lyndon. *"First, let her think she's having her way. And second, let her have it."*

What Are You Trying to Say?

Lyndon Johnson claimed that there are, essentially, two kinds of speeches. The first is the **Mother Hubbard** speech, which covers everything but touches nothing. The second is the **Bikini** speech, which covers only the essential points.

When in Rome...

As Majority Leader in the 1950s, **Lyndon Johnson** often held the Senate in session well into the night. During one **arduous** day, Johnson got his fellow senators to confirm an ambassador, approve a Federal Trade Commissioner, and pass **90** bills—in less than five hours! One exhausted Senator whispered to a colleague, *"What's all the rush?* **Rome** *wasn't built in a day."*

"No," his colleague agreed wearily, *"but* **Lyndon Johnson** *wasn't the* **foreman** *on* **that** *job!"*

LBJ the boy

A Good Match

The parents of **Lyndon Johnson** were widely regarded as a good match in the Texas of their time. His father was a relatively well off farmer/teacher/politician. His mother, Rebecca Baines, was the **only female graduate** of a college in their rural Texas county. One neighbor approved the match, saying, *"The Baineses have the brains, and the Johnsons have the guts. The Bainses are intelligent, but they can't put things over. The Johnsons can put things over."*

Opening the Cabinet Doors

On January 13, 1966, Lyndon Johnson appointed Robert C. Weaver to be Secretary of Housing and Urban Development. Weaver was the first **African-American** to hold a Cabinet post.

Born: *Yorba Linda CA, January 9, 1913*
Died: *New York City, April 22, 1994*

Tricky Dick

One Too Many "Firsts"?

Richard Nixon was the first President to visit **China** while in office.

He was also the first to visit **Moscow**.

Among the many "firsts" that Nixon could claim, and did, was being the first President to visit **all 50 U.S. states**.

His **resignation** as President was his final first.

Casting Call

Richard Nixon was cast in a **play** at a small local theater, where he met high school teacher Pat Ryan. Apparently, Nixon was struck by the grace and beauty of the young teacher, who had actually had bit parts in **Hollywood** films. He asked her to marry him in the course of their first date. Pat thought it was distinctly **odd**, *"I thought he was **nuts** or something,"* she said succinctly.

Even the Pros Get It Wrong

On November 6, **1962**, after being defeated in the California gubernatorial election, future President **Richard Nixon** announced to reporters, **"You won't have Nixon to kick around anymore, because, Gentlemen, this is my last press conference."**

Slippery Gulch's Most Famous Citizen

During two summer vacations while he was in high school, **Richard Nixon** worked in Prescott, Arizona, as a barker for the **Wheel of Chance** at the "Slippery Gulch Rodeo."

Playing Checkers

Ice now, but soon to be slush.

Richard Nixon gave one of the best speeches of his, or any other American politician's, career when he was accused of having a "**slush fund**" during his first Vice Presidential campaign in 1952. Nixon bought television air time and described his family's modest finances. He concluded with a bit of political theater which has rarely been surpassed. He said, *"We did get something—a gift…It was a little cocker spaniel dog in a crate that had been sent all the way from Texas. Black and white spotted. And our little girl—Tricia, the six-year-old—named it **Checkers**. And you know, the kids, like all kids, love the dog and I just want to say this right now, that regardless of what they say about it, we're gonna keep it."*

Wish I'd Said That!

John F. Kennedy defeated **Richard Nixon** for the White House in 1960 by a very narrow margin. After listening to Kennedy's famous **inaugural address**, Richard Nixon graciously complimented one of Kennedy's speechwriters, Ted Sorensen. He admitted that there were things in the address that Nixon wished he had said himself. Sorensen was interested and asked which of Kennedy's words Nixon wished he had said. Nixon replied, *"the part beginning with 'I do solemnly swear….'"*

Born: *Omaha NE, July 14, 1913*
Died: *Rancho Mirage CA,*
December 26, 2006

Jerry

Presidents on Other Presidents

Gerald Ford was a great admirer of President Harry Truman. Truman, Ford said

66 ...had guts, he was plain-talking, he had no illusions about being a great intellectual, but he seemed to make the right decisions. 99

From One President to Another

Lyndon Johnson on Jerry Ford:

66 Jerry is a nice guy but he played too much football with his helmet off. 99

The Only Time a King Was President

Once upon a time a **King** became President of the United States. When he was still very young, his parents were divorced, and he was adopted by his stepfather. Instead of being called **Leslie King, Jr.**, he became **Gerald Ford, Jr.** And everyone lived happily ever after!

I Just Got Here Myself

Shortly after he became President, **Gerald Ford** was showing a visitor around the White House. A large painting caught the visitor's attention. *"Is that a* **Gilbert Stuart***?"* he asked the President. *"I don't know,"* replied Ford. *"I haven't been here long enough."*

Keeping Expectations Low

On accepting his appointment as Vice-President, **Gerald Ford** made a short speech during which he reminded his audience, *"Remember, I'm a* **Ford***, not a Lincoln."*

The First

Gerald Ford is the **first** President not to have been elected at all! He was appointed to complete the term of the resigned Vice President Spiro Agnew. Then **Richard Nixon** resigned, and Ford succeeded him as President.

Taking the Long View

Betty Ford was asked how to be a political wife. *"I was very unprepared to be a political wife but I didn't worry because I really didn't think he was going to win!"*

A Royal Remark

To mark 200 years of American Independence, Britain's **Queen Elizabeth** paid a state visit to the White House. The Ford's son, Jack, an informal young man, realized that he did not have studs for his formal shirt. He decided to borrow a set from his father. He got onto the White House elevator, hair uncombed, his shirt hanging open, only to discover to his horror that his fellow passengers were his parents and the Queen herself. Mrs. Ford was deeply embarrassed, but the Queen, with her famous tact, observed quietly, *"I have one just like that!"*

Honesty Is Not Always the Best Policy

Gerald Ford delivered a standard stump speech in Omaha, Nebraska. At a post-speech reception, the President was shaking hands and chatting amiably with the crowd. One particularly sweet-looking elderly woman said to him, *"I hear you gave a speech here tonight."* Realizing that she had missed the speech, the President hastened to reassure her, **"Oh, it was nothing."** The woman agreed sweetly, *"Yes, that's what I heard."*

The World Is Watching

Gerald Ford loved to play golf, and once he was able to play with hockey superstar Gordie Howe. Howe graciously conceded a two-foot putt to the President, but Ford insisted on playing it to be sportsmanlike. As luck (or skill) would have it, he missed. Howe shrugged and said, *"We won't count that one."* Ford indicated the press photographers, *"Maybe you won't,"* he said, *"but **THEY** will."*

91

Born: *Plains GA, October 1, 1924*

Jimmy

Raise Your Sights, Midshipman!

Jimmy Carter had not always aspired to the presidency. At one time, his ambitions were somewhat more modest. *"When I was a midshipman at Annapolis,"* he acknowledges, *"the only thing I wanted to be was Chief of Naval Operations."* Talk about overachieving!

An Affair to Remember

Jimmy Carter had staunch **Southern Baptist** beliefs, so reporters would often ask him questions about his moral positions. One reporter famously asked, *"How would you feel if you were told that your **daughter** was having an affair."* Carter shook his head sadly, *"Shocked and overwhelmed,"* he said, *"But then, she's only seven years old!"*

Well, Let's Sea!

While President, **Jimmy Carter** was discussing international affairs with reporters. When the official transcript of the meeting was released, there were a number of references to **"a GNC."** This was a new one even to the most seasoned reporters, and they were hard put to discover this new agency or even what its initials represented. The next day, the White House Press Office, rather red-faced, explained that "a GNC" should have been "**Aegean Sea**."

The Cat's Meow!

Jimmy Carter faced the aftermath of the great **oil crisis** of the 1970s. He was deeply concerned and wanted Americans to begin to plan for a future without oil. He introduced an energy-savings program, which he weightily named **The Moral Equivalent of War**. Well, it was not well received, and those who disliked it soon began to call it by its acronym, **MEOW**.

Attack Rabbit

Jimmy Carter is the only President who was ever attacked by a rabbit. The President was rowing his rowboat on a pond on his Plains, Georgia, peanut farm. He saw a large animal, plainly in distress, swimming determinedly toward his boat. He saw that it was a rabbit, but not a cute little bunny, rather a large, and apparently **deranged, hare**. The President was unsure what to do, but he was certain that he did not wish to have the rabbit sharing his boat, especially since it was hissing and showing its teeth. Carter pushed the animal away from the boat and all ended well—until a newspaper reporter got the story.

Grrrrr...

He Draws a Crowd

Jimmy Carter has been active in volunteer organizations since leaving the White House. One of his activities is working with **Habitat for Humanity** to build affordable houses. He recalled the time the group planned to build houses in Mumbai, India. The organizers had figured the job would take five days. However, Hollywood star **Brad Pitt** arrived to help. *"It took only four days because Brad Pitt showed up, and we were inundated with volunteers,"* the former President joked. *"And he [Brad Pitt] really worked, I might say,"* Carter added.

I'll Take a Half Dozen with Jimmies

Want your son to be President? Name him James. **James Earl Carter** is simply the most recent James to reach the Oval Office. His predecessors (in reverse order) were **James Garfield**, **James Buchanan**, **James Polk**, **James Monroe**, and **James Madison**.

James Garfield   James Buchanan   James Polk   James Monroe   James Madison

93

Born: *Tampico IL, February 6, 1911*
Died: *Los Angeles CA, June 5, 2004*

The Great Communicator

Presidents on the Presidency

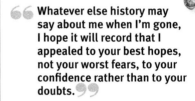

❝ Politics is supposed to be the second oldest profession. I have come to realize that it bears a close resemblance to the first. ❞

— Ronald Reagan

Presidents on their Record

❝ Whatever else history may say about me when I'm gone, I hope it will record that I appealed to your best hopes, not your worst fears, to your confidence rather than to your doubts. ❞

— Ronald Reagan

Using a Reference

Ronald Reagan arrived late to a Cabinet meeting. He said he had seen a young man on television, who had **saved** someone who had fallen in front of a train. Reagan asked his staff to locate the young man because he wanted to congratulate him. The young hero was delighted but he mentioned that the phone call was going to make him late for a **job interview**. Reagan asked for the prospective employer's phone number. He called the work number and asked them to give the young man a job. They did—and on the hero's own merits—but a **presidential reference** can't hurt!

The Personal Touch

Presidents receive vast quantities of mail every day. (Even presidential pets seem to get about **100 letters** a week!) A lot of this mail comes from private citizens and **Ronald Reagan** took that seriously. He had his staff select around fifty letters each weekend. He took them with him and read them privately. And then he answered almost all of them….by hand!

Well, There Was No Rehearsal

Ronald Reagan was shot by John Hinckley as he left the Washington Hilton on March 30, 1981. Nancy Reagan was working in the White House and quickly rushed to the hospital to be at her husband's side. At this point, Mrs. Reagan knew only that her husband had been shot, but no further details were known. As she rushed into her husband's presence, he looked up and said sheepishly, "**Honey, I forgot to duck**!"

Reagan on His Age

Ronald Reagan was the oldest man to become President. During the election campaign of 1980, much was made of his **age**. Reagan approached the issue squarely, "*I want you to know that also I will not make age an issue of this campaign. I am not going to exploit, for political purposes, my opponent's youth and inexperience.*" At the time, his opponent was 56- year-old Walter Mondale, who had been a senator and Vice President.

Presidents on Other Presidents

Ronald Reagan was able to make fun of his own age and also of his political opponent, Lloyd Bentsen after the latter told Dan Quayle that he was "**no John Kennedy**." "*This fellow they've nominated (Senator Lloyd Bentsen) claims he's the new Thomas Jefferson. Well, let me tell you something; I knew Thomas Jefferson. He was a friend of mine and Governor…. You're no Thomas Jefferson!*"

95

Born: *Milton MA, June 12, 1924*

Bush 41

Presidents on the Presidency

> 66 I do not like broccoli. And I haven't liked it since I was a little kid, and my mother made me eat it. And I'm President of the United States, and I'm not going to eat any more broccoli. 99

— George H.W. Bush

The First

George H. W. Bush was the first President who had previously been Director of the Central Intelligence Agency.

Well, THAT'S a Relief!

> 66 I have opinions of my own, strong opinions, but I don't always agree with them. 99

— George H. W. Bush

Up in the Air

George H. W. Bush has an unusual way to celebrate his birthdays. On his 75th birthday in 1999, he jumped out of an airplane (with a parachute, of course). His wife, Barbara Bush, was neither impressed nor amused. Then, he did it again five years later to celebrate his 80th birthday. And THAT was the last straw! *"If the jump doesn't kill him, I will!"* Mrs. Bush announced.

From Prep School to the Pacific

...we here highly resolve that these de shall not have died in vain...

REMEMBER DEC. 7th!

George H. W. Bush was the oldest son of a U.S. Senator, Prescott Bush from Connecticut. The younger Bush was in school when the Japanese attacked **Pearl Harbor** on December 7, 1941. Young Bush immediately volunteered for the navy. At the age of 18 he became the **youngest naval aviator** in US history up to that time.

A Small Carrier Group

George H. W. Bush is the only living President who has an **aircraft carrier** named after him. Other Presidents who have been so honored are George Washington, Abraham Lincoln, Theodore Roosevelt, Dwight Eisenhower, Harry Truman, and Ronald Reagan.

A Close Call

In the air war over the Pacific, **George H. W. Bush's** plane was shot down. He and the other surviving crew member bailed out. The other crewman's parachute failed to open. Bush waited for rescue on an inflated raft for four hours. For his heroism, he received the **Distinguished Flying Cross** and three Air Medals.

Lip Reading for Beginners

Political pundits say that one offhanded remark may have cost **George H. W. Bush** reelection in 1992. The President was trying to hold the line on taxes in spite of a looming federal budget deficit. "**Read my lips**," he famously said. *"No new taxes!"* Unfortunately, he DID agree to new taxes, and the quote came back to haunt him during his reelection campaign.

East Meets West

George H. W. Bush is well remembered for having vomited into the lap of Prime Minister Kiichi Miyazawa of Japan during a state dinner in 1992. What is less well known is that the Japanese invented a term for the event: *busshu-suru*, meaning literally *"to do a Bush,"* but as slang *"to vomit in public."* So that's what you call what happens after a Frat house party!

Born: *Hope AR, August 19, 1946*

The Comeback Kid

Presidents on the Presidency

66 Well, I can meet anybody I want to! 99

— **William Jefferson Clinton**

Interestingly, this is the same remark President **John F. Kennedy** made when asked what he liked about being President.

Well, It Would Be a Change

Bill Clinton was asked about the memoir he was writing, *"A lot of presidential memoirs, they say, are dull and self-serving. I hope mine is interesting and self-serving."*

Presidents on Other Presidents

Bill Clinton was deeply touched by the kind remarks made by his successor President **George W. Bush** when the official **White House portraits** of the Clintons were unveiled.

Clinton said,

66 I especially thanked him for mentioning my mother and my father-in-law. And he reminded me that I had been very generous to his father. I never minded President Bush not liking me very much because I defeated his father. He loves his **daddy**. And he ought to love his daddy. 99

A Gilded Cage

66 The White House: I don't know whether it's the finest public housing in America or the crown jewel of the prison system. 99

— **Bill Clinton**

Mr. President, Meet a Future President

Bill Clinton was visiting the White House with a group of other boys from the Boys' Nation Conference in 1963. President **John F. Kennedy** greeted the boys and shook their hands. Neither man could have suspected that, one day, this boy from Arkansas would occupy the **Oval Office**.

Cattiness? At the White House!

Bill Clinton's cat **Socks** had an exciting new life at the White House during the President's first term. However, his life changed abruptly in the new term when a dog named **Buddy** arrived at the White House. Socks, said First Lady Hillary Rodham Clinton, *"...despised Buddy from first sight, instantly and forever."* The President admitted ruefully, *"I did better with... the Palestinians and the Israelis than I've done with Socks and Buddy."* Like some previous White House pets, Socks has a book *Socks Goes to Washington* by Michael O'Donoghue. However, Socks is the first White House pet to appear on a **postage stamp** (for the Central African Republic).

The President at Work

Bill Clinton was campaigning for governor in Arkansas in 1982. He was walking up the main street of a small town. A pickup truck pulled up to a traffic light with **three dogs** in the truck bed. Clinton started walking toward the truck. As he walked, he whispered to his aide, *"What kind of dogs are those? How old are they?"* His aide replied in a whisper, *"They look like bird dogs. About three years old, I'd say."* Clinton smiled at the driver of the pickup and said, *"Those are great-looking bird dogs you got there. How old are they, about three years?"* The pickup driver's face lit up in a smile. Here was a governor who really knew his **bird dogs**! Count one more vote for Governor Clinton!

Born: *New Haven CT, July 6, 1946*

Dubya

A President on His Presidency

66 They misunderestimated me. 99

— George W. Bush

Presidents on Other Presidents

66 It hurts much more if your son's President. My husband.... he's in agony half the time. 99

— Barbara Bush

A Hidden Talent

George W. Bush is a **poet**, although few Americans know it. This example is a poem he wrote for First Lady Laura Bush when she was in Europe.

Roses are red

    Violets are blue

      Oh my, lump in the bed

      How I've missed you.

      Bluer am I

      Seeing you kissed by that charming French guy.

      The dogs and the cat, they missed you too

      Barney's still mad you dropped him, he ate your shoe

      The distance, my dear, has been such a barrier

Next time you want an adventure, just land on a carrier.

Locking the Cabinet Doors

George W. Bush prizes punctuality. He does not like to be late, and he does not like others to be late for meetings with him. The President once **locked** Secretary of State **Colin Powell** out of a Cabinet meeting because he was late.

So That's What Diplomats Whisper About

George W. Bush attended a meeting of the UN General Assembly along with his Secretary of State Condoleezza Rice. They were seen whispering intently to each other during the meeting. Now the truth can be revealed. Bush had slipped Rice a note on which he had written, *"I think I may need a **bathroom break**? Is this possible?"* Presumably, he meant is it possible in diplomacy to be excused. He must have known whether or not he needed a bathroom break.

Making Change

Police in Kentucky were able to apprehend several people who successfully used a phony **$200 bill**. (That's right, there is no $200 bill!) The phony bill had a picture of the White House on the back with a sign on the lawn, "**We like broccoli**." (See President George H.W. Bush) The front of the bill featured a smiling photo of President **George W. Bush**.

You Mean She's a He?

George W. Bush praised Libyan dissident **Fathi Jahmi** as one of the world's **leading women reformers**. His remarks were timed to mark *International Women's Week* in 2004. Bush pointed out that Jahmi had spent two years in prison for her defense of civil liberties in Libya. There was only one problem: Jahmi is a man.

Fit for a Queen

George W. Bush has a dislike of formal events. During a reception at the White House during the administration of his father, **George H.W. Bush,** the president-yet-to-be was chatting with **Queen Elizabeth II**. Young Bush admitted he hadn't been so successful in life and, if the truth were to be told, allowed that he had been sort of his **family's black sheep**. Then to continue the conversation, he asked Her Majesty, *"Who's yours?"* First Lady Barbara Bush firmly intervened, *"Don't answer that!"* she ordered.

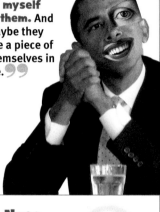

Born: *Honolulu HI, August 4, 1961*

Bama

Presidents on the Presidency

" All of these different strands in me – the black, the white, the African – all of that contributed directly to my success because when I meet people, I see a piece of myself in them. And maybe they see a piece of themselves in me. "

His Higher Power

Barack Obama was asked by a group of Illinois politicians to run for an state senate seat. Obama says he did what every black man does when asked to make an important decision; he prayed about it and he asked his **wife**.

Winning by a Nose

While running for President in 2008 against **Senator Hillary Clinton**, **Barack Obama** paused in the middle of a speech in Dallas to blow his nose. The Texas crowd cheered noisily for his efforts! Obama then mused, *"If I can get cheers just by blowing my nose, maybe Hillary is putting too much emphasis on my supposed eloquence!"* he quipped.

Presidents on Other Presidents

Barack Obama responded to press questions about the effect former President **Bill Clinton** would have when he campaigned for his wife, **Hillary Rodham Clinton** during the 2008 Democratic primaries. Obama observed,

> ❝ **My understanding is that President Clinton is not on the ballot.** ❞

Out of His League

Barack Obama was challenged to a **bowling match** during the 2008 presidential campaign. His challenger, Roxanne Hart, easily took the lead over the presidential candidate and a friend, named Casey. Obama's first effort was a gutter ball, but he promised the crowd he was "**just warming up**." The game went south from there. Finally, Obama announced that his goal was to beat his friend, Casey. *"I can't beat Roxanne,"* he admitted with a grin!

The First

Barack Obama is the first **African American** to be elected President. The Reverend Jesse Jackson ran for the Democratic nomination in 1984 and again in 1988, but **Barack Obama** is the first African American to be nominated by a major political party.

A Lifelong Dream

During the 2008 Democratic presidential campaign, Senator Hillary Clinton accused **Barack Obama** of wanting to be President even when he was in **kindergarten**. The charge didn't get much traction, but Obama worked it into a later speech. When he became the Democratic front-runner, he remarked, *"This feels good. It's just like I imagined it when I was talking to my kindergarten teacher."*

What's in a Name

Barack Obama has often remarked that his name causes comment. People insist on mispronouncing it, he has been called **Baracko Bama**, **Alabama**, and **Yo' Mama**.

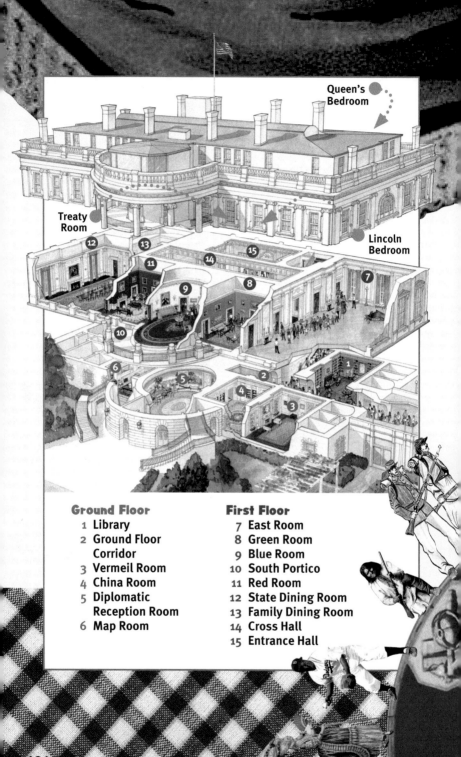

Queen's
Bedroom

Treaty
Room

Lincoln
Bedroom

Ground Floor

First Floor

White House Life

Growing Into Its Role

The **White House** must have seemed overly grand in 1801. In fact, it was the largest house in the United States for its first 70 years! Today the White House encloses 55,000 square feet on six floors. There are **132 rooms** and **35 bathrooms**, 147 windows, 412 doors, 28 working fireplaces, 8 staircases, and 3 elevators. It takes 570 gallons of white paint just to cover the outside walls! The oldest Presidential object in the White House is Gilbert Stuart's portrait of **George Washington** (see below).

She Thought She Had Him

Martha Washington knew **Gilbert Stuart** was America's best portrait artist. She also knew that Stuart had a serious drinking problem and was completely unreliable about delivery. He had previously made quite a lot of money by selling copies before delivering an original.

Martha was a smart businesswoman, so she insisted that Stuart deliver the portrait as soon as it was finished, or she would not pay for it. The result was one of the finest portraits of our first President.

However, Stuart had cleverly left a part of the collar unpainted so that he could honestly tell Martha (for months!) that the painting was "not yet finished." This gave him time to knock off his "hundred dollar bills" (as he called them)—more than 200 copies of the painting.

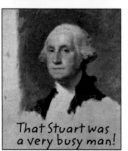

That Stuart was a very busy man!

A Secret Plan

Irish-born architect, James Hoban, submitted the winning design for the White House. One losing design was signed A. Z., who turned out to be none other than Thomas Jefferson!

The First

The first President to live in the White House was **John Adams**, who moved in on November 1, 1800. Adams wrote to his wife in Philadelphia, *"I pray heaven to bestow the best of blessings on this house and all that shall hereafter inhabit it. May none but wise and honest men ever rule under this roof."* President **Franklin D. Roosevelt** ordered these words engraved on the mantelpiece of the State Dining Room.

Hot Time in the Old Town

Every American knows that Dolley Madison saved Washington's portrait and other valuables before **British troops burned the White House** in 1814. What fewer Americans know is that President **James Madison's** dinner was calmly eaten by British officers before they torched the Executive Mansion. What very few Americans know is that Washington was burned in retaliation for the American burning of Upper Canada's capital, York (today's Toronto).

A Formal Drying Room

The **East Room** of the White House has been the scene of many grand receptions over the years. The first event held there by Mrs. John Adams, however, was not for dignitaries. Abigail Adams wrote of the event to her daughter, *"We have not the least fence, yard, or other convenience without, and the great unfinished audience room,* **I make a drying room of, to hang the clothes in.** *"*

She'd Had Practice

Dolley Madison was one of the most popular First Ladies in American history. In fact, Dolley was First Lady for TWO Presidents. Prior to the two terms of her husband, James, she had served as official White House hostess for his predecessor, **Thomas Jefferson**, a widower. Among her innovations was **ice cream** at White House dinners. (That is why **cherry vanilla** is still called White House ice cream today!) Even after leaving the White House, and in spite of increasing poverty, Dolley Madison remained at the center of social life in Washington until her death in 1849.

The First

Martha Washington was called simply "Lady Washington." There is reason to believe that **"First Lady"** was a title in use informally for many years, and may first have referred to Dolley Madison.

In 1877, a newspaper referred to Lucy Webb Hayes as "the First Lady of the Land." The term caught on and became an official title for a presidential hostess (Widowed presidents and those whose wives were too ill asked a close female relative to fill the role.)

The title "First Lady" is an American invention, but it can now describe the wife of any head of state. Interestingly, many American First Ladies have said privately that they dislike the title.

Madame Lafayette, We Are Here

During the French Revolution, the wife of the **Marquis de Lafayette**, was imprisoned and awaiting the **guillotine**. Her mother, sister, and grandmother had already been beheaded.

A carriage drew up to the prison gate. A crowd gathered, wondering about this visitor speaking to Madame de Lafayette. **Mrs. James Monroe**, wife of the American Minister to France, had come at her husband's request to demonstrate publicly America's sympathy for the prisoner. (Monroe's official position prevented his coming himself.)

Madame Lafayette was grateful, and the French government took the hint. Shortly after, and as a direct result of Elizabeth Monroe's visit, Adrienne de Lafayette was **released**.

A Rose by Any Other Name...

John Tyler's beautiful second wife, Julia Gardiner Tyler, was called "The Rose of Long Island." She herself said that she **"reigned"** during the final eight months of the Tyler presidency. She received guests at the White House, seated on a dais and attended by four "ladies in waiting." Her final White House ball boasted **3000 guests**! She said to a friend, "*Nothing appears to delight the President more than...to hear people sing my praises.*"

No Wonder He Had Only One Term

James Polk's wife, Sarah Childress Polk, was a no-nonsense kind of woman. She was scrupulously honest and upright; she wouldn't even accept bouquets from the national greenhouse. Mrs. Polk forbade drinking in the White House, and card-playing, and dancing! The reaction of visitors to her White House is not recorded, but her husband served only one term.

A Fixer-Upper!

Running water was piped into the White House for the first time in 1833. Central heating was installed in 1837. Gaslights were first used in 1848. President **Franklin Pierce** took advantage of hot water newly piped into the second floor to install the first bathtub in 1853. Electric lights appeared in 1890. (The **Benjamin Harrisons** were afraid to touch the light switches!) An electric elevator was installed in 1898 for Mrs. William McKinley, an invalid.

They Bought Round Trip Tickets

Frances Folsom married **Grover Cleveland** in a White House ceremony in 1886, when the bride was 21, our youngest First Lady. When Cleveland lost his reelection bid, they gathered the White House staff. *"Take good care of the place,"* Mrs. Cleveland told them. *"We'll be back."* Four years later, they returned in triumph, accompanied by new baby, Ruth Cleveland. (For whom, it is said, the Baby Ruth candy bar, was named.)

On a Roll

Lucy Webb Hayes was the first college graduate to become First Lady. She understood a lot outside textbooks, too! When Congressmen complained that the annual **Easter egg-rolling** festivities were ruining the grass around the Capitol, Lucy Webb Hayes had the activity moved to the White House lawn. The children had their egg rolling, the Congressmen had their grass, and the White House had the start of a popular tradition.

Out With the Old

A man of exquisite (and expensive) taste, **Chester A. Arthur** refused to move into the White House in 1881 until 81 years' worth of its shabbier furniture and ornaments were removed. So, **24 wagonloads** of historic furniture and hopeless junk were carted off to be sold at auction.

"Elegant Arthur" then had the interior of the mansion redecorated and furnished by **Louis Comfort Tiffany**, New York's most stylish decorator. (And historians have been looking for lost White House treasures ever since!)

On Her Toes?

He was a lanky, intense young lawyer. She was from a wealthy Kentucky family, and her sister had just married the son of the governor of Illinois. They met in Springfield, Illinois, in 1839. She was the belle of this particular ball, flirting and dancing with all the eligible young beaus. (Including an up-and-coming young politician named Stephen Douglas!)

Finally, the young lawyer, who was not noted for his social graces, got up the courage to ask her to dance. **Abraham Lincoln** approached **Mary Todd** nervously and said, *"Miss Todd, I want to dance with you in the worst way."* She commented later, *"He certainly did!"*

Not a Rave Review

Some White House occupants have been less than impressed by the Executive Mansion.

Alice Roosevelt Longworth, **Theodore Roosevelt's** outspoken daughter, remarked that the décor of the White House was *"late Grant, early Pullman."*

However, Roosevelt and **his family** enjoyed their lives in the White House. They had obstacle races, pillow fights, and other high-spirited games. One British diplomat remarked, *"You must remember that the President is about six."*

A newspaper reporter once tried to pump the youngest Roosevelt, Quentin, for backstairs gossip about the President. In a convincingly world-weary voice, the seven-year-old drawled, *"I see him sometimes, but I know nothing of his family life."*

The White House Gets a Name

It was popularly referred to as the White House from the very beginning. (And it was painted white from the beginning, too!) It has also been called the President's Palace, the Executive Mansion, and the President's House, but the building had no official name until **Theodore Roosevelt** took up residence. His presidential **stationery** proudly proclaimed "The White House." Today's White House stationery design, with the words White House centered on the page, are a product of the **Franklin Roosevelt** administration.

Great Scott, Harrison!

Caroline Scott Harrison began the White House collection of presidential china patterns. Today's White House China Collection has representative pieces from every President since Washington, thanks to the efforts of Mrs. Harrison and later First Ladies. Mrs. Harrison also put up the first **Christmas tree** at the White House. Oh, and she also found time to help found the Daughters of the American Revolution and to serve as the organization's first president.

Ponying Up

When **Theodore Roosevelt's** son Archie was put to bed with measles, his younger brother Quentin knew that seeing his **pony** would be just the thing to cheer the invalid. So Quentin brought the pony up to the sickroom level in the White House elevator. Everyone agreed that the pony had behaved very well, and Archie was delighted to see his four-legged friend!

There Goes the Neighborhood

Edith Roosevelt was regarded as even shrewder than her husband, Teddy. She once asked the French ambassador why France could not copy the example of Canada and the United States. *"We have a three-thousand-mile, unfortified, peaceful frontier. You people arm yourselves to the teeth."* The ambassador heaved a great sigh, *"Ah, Madame, perhaps we could exchange neighbors."*

Reoriented

Helen Taft loved flowers and gardens. On a visit to Tokyo, Mrs. Taft was impressed with the beautiful **cherry trees** in bloom. By 1912, Mrs. Taft was First Lady. She arranged for the gift of 3,000 Japanese cherry trees to the nation's capital. Her cherry trees continue to blossom spectacularly around the Tidal Basin every spring.

The Oval Office

The "Oval Office" has become almost a cliché for the President himself, but this room was not in the original White House. In fact, before 1909, most Presidents worked in one of the upstairs rooms. The Oval Office was created for **William Howard Taft** during a White House renovation.

The **"Resolute Desk"** in the Oval Office was a gift to the President from Britain's Queen Victoria in 1880. It has been used by every President since **Rutherford B. Hayes**. (Except for Presidents **Johnson**, **Nixon**, and **Ford**). **John Kennedy, Jr.,** used to play under the desk as a toddler, but he called the desk "my house."

Tell That to the President

On one occasion, President and Mrs. **Calvin Coolidge** were touring an agricultural station. While Coolidge was away for a moment, the farmer happened to tell Mrs. Coolidge that his rooster mated constantly. Mrs. Coolidge said drily, *"Tell that to the President."*

When the farmer told the President what Mrs. Coolidge had said, the President asked, *"Is it always with the same hen?"*

"Oh no," the farmer assured him. *"With different hens."*

The President smiled, *"Tell that to Mrs. Coolidge."*

To this day, scientists refer to the biological ability of male animals to wish to mate with multiple females "the Coolidge Effect."

And It Wasn't Even May Day

Eleanor Roosevelt was asked to escort a group of Soviet diplomats to a parade in New York City. As a group of uniformed youths marched past the reviewing stand, the diplomats remarked, *"The military!"*

Mrs. Roosevelt shook her head and told them these were **Boy Scouts**. Then a group of men in uniform passed. *"Military?"* the diplomats asked. She shook her head, *"The Fire Department,"* she said.

Then an open car came by with a group of elderly men in rather moth-eaten uniforms. Mrs. Roosevelt smiled sweetly and said, *"The military."*

Girls Will Be Girls

Woodrow Wilson's daughters, **Margaret**, **Jessie**, and **Eleanor**, liked to join White House guided tours, keeping their identities secret from the tourists. As the guide led visitors through the Executive Mansion, the girls would embarrass their fellow tour members by making loud and highly critical remarks about President Wilson's daughters.

Margaret and Jessie Wilson

Boy Scouts running down Fifth Avenue

Taking All Prizes

To a group of Nobel Prize winners attending a White House dinner, **John Kennedy** made this toast:

"I believe this is the most extraordinary collection of talent, of human knowledge,

*that has ever been gathered together at the White House, with the possible exception of when **Thomas Jefferson** dined alone."*

She Brought Down the House

The White House was pretty run down by the time **Harry S Truman** became President. Workmen had sawed through load-bearing beams, floors had sagged, and ceilings were weak.

Even Congress realized that something had to be done the day that the leg of Margaret Truman's piano came through the ceiling of the Family Dining Room. The Trumans moved out, the contractors moved in, and the mansion was rebuilt to last another 150 years.

Worth Waiting For...

Jackie Kennedy was famous for her style and glamour. During a state visit to **Paris**, she dazzled the not-so-easily-dazzled French crowds. **John Kennedy** always loved her crowd appeal. At the final banquet of the tour, he began his remarks with the very gallant statement, *"I am the man who accompanied Jacqueline Kennedy to Paris, and I have enjoyed it."*

That's What You Get for Your $20

Harry Truman wanted to build a second-floor porch on the White House. The funds ($10,000) were available, and the porch was added. There was only one problem. In 1948, the back of the **$20 bill** carried a picture of the South Front of the White House. A new plate had to be engraved to show the new porch.

BH: Before Harry

AH: After Harry

113

> No, no dear! I didn't MEAN you!

Now There's a Headline!

Thelma Ryan Nixon was always called "Pat" because she was born the day before Saint Patrick's Day. This became a problem only once. Her husband gave a speech in which he declared that much remained to be done, and Republicans should not rest on their laurels. The American people would not want the GOP to stand pat on its previous accomplishments. The next day, banner headlines greeted newspaper readers, **"Can't Stand Pat," Says Richard Nixon."**

There Was a Long Intermission

Several performers have given concerts at the White House for more than one President. **Pablo Casals**, the famous Spanish cellist, played at the White House twice. The first time, in 1904, was for President **Theodore Roosevelt.** The second time was 57 years later, for President **John F. Kennedy.**

I'd Rather Not...

A young Houston reporter named **Dan Rather** was interviewing **Lyndon Johnson** at his **ranch** in Texas. Johnson lost his temper at the young reporter and ordered him to leave his house. The shaken Rather was at his car when his thoughts were interrupted.

Lady Bird Johnson had come ro soothe Rather's hurt feelings. She shrugged the whole incident off, *"That's just the way Lyndon sometimes is."*

The Princess and the Frog

One of the most glamorous events at the White House occurred in 1985, when Britain's **Princess Diana** visited. Dazzling with her good looks and considerable charm, the Princess apparently had just one request: to dance with fellow-guest John Travolta. First Lady Nancy Reagan took the film star aside and explained the Princess's request. Travolta reassured Mrs. Reagan, *"We're good. I can do this."* Later the actor confessed that, as he took the Princess onto the dance floor, he felt *"...like a frog who had been turned into a prince."*

The Best Man for the Job

"Somewhere out there in this audience may even be someone who will one day follow in my footsteps, and preside over the White House as the President's spouse. I wish him well."

Barbara Bush

The "Dog House"

Harry Truman famously remarked, *'If you want a friend in Washington, get a dog!'* **Washington, Jefferson, Madison, Monroe, William Henry Harrison, Tyler, Taylor,** and **Polk** had dogs. **Jackson, Lincoln,** both **Teddy** and **Franklin Roosevelt** had dogs. So did **Wilson, Harding, Coolidge** and **Hoover, Eisenhower, Kennedy, Johnson, Nixon, Ford, Reagan, Clinton,** and both **Bushes.**

President **George H.W. Bush's** springer spaniel, **Millie**, was the first White House pet to write a book of memoirs, *Millie's Book: As Dictated to Barbara Bush*. Millie's son, Spot Fetcher, moved back into the White House with George H.W. Bush's son, President **George W. Bush**.

But the dog who had it best was Rex, a Cavalier King Charles Spaniel belonging to the **Ronald Reagans**. Rex lived in an elegant doghouse with framed pictures of the President and the First Lady. This doggy dacha was designed by Theo Hayes, who happens to be the great-grandson of President **Rutherford B. Hayes**. Right from the beginning, the dogs have been going to the White House. Or you could put it the other way, if you prefer.

Millie Bush

Getting Away From It All

First Lady **Hillary Rodham Clinton** was surrounded in the White House. There were times when she simply wanted to be alone and unrecognized.

She discovered that she could **bicycle** incognito if she pushed her hair up under a baseball cap and wore dark glasses. Her Secret Service detail dutifully followed on bicycles, but at a discreet distance.

One day the First Lady was enjoying her ride when a group of Japanese tourists waved at her and held up their camera. *"Uh-oh,"* she thought. *"They've recognized me."*

With a sigh, she stopped her bike and smiled. The Japanese smiled back and asked her if she would take **their picture**!

The First

First Lady **Hillary Rodham Clinton** is the first presidential spouse to win an office on her own. She was elected to the **Senate** from the state of New York in 2000. In 2008, Senator Clinton ran for the presidency in her own right. She lost her campaign for the nomination, but she proved that a woman can be a serious candidate for the Oval Office.

Free Speech

First Lady **Laura Bush** says she learned the hard way that it was not a good idea to criticize her husband's speeches. After one speech while he was still a Texas politician, he asked for her opinion. She reluctantly admitted that she didn't think the speech was too good. Bush was so astonished that he drove into the garage wall! Anyway the First Lady points out, by the time she is asked, it is too late.....the President has already given the speech!

The White House Kitchen

These are actual White House recipes. But be careful! They may give you a taste for the Presidency!

Rosalynn Carter's Peanut Soup

Jimmy Carter's election spurred a real boom in the peanut industry. Rich and creamy, this peanut soup, a favorite recipe of Mrs. Carter, is deliciously worthy of the White House table.

¼ cup minced onion
1 tbsp butter or margarine
½ cup smooth peanut butter
1 can (10½ oz) cream of chicken soup
2 soup cans of milk
¼ cup chopped peanuts (optional)

- Melt butter and sauté onion until transparent and soft (do not brown).
- Stir in peanut butter, and when heated through, gradually blend in soup and milk.
- Add chopped, salted peanuts if desired. Stir until smooth and heat until just before boiling. (Do not boil.)
- Serve at once, garnished with additional chopped peanuts, parsley or dash of paprika.

Makes 4-6 servings

Martha Washington's Crab Soup

Martha Washington insisted on boiling her own crabs for this recipe. Today, it is just as good (and a lot easier) to use canned or frozen crab.

1 cup crab meat
1 tbsp butter
1½ tbsp flour
3 hard-boiled eggs, mashed with fork
1 lemon rind, grated
dash salt
dash pepper
4 cups milk
½ cup heavy cream
½ cup sherry
dash Worcestershire sauce

- Bring the milk to a boil.
- Combine butter, flour, mashed eggs, lemon rind, salt and pepper in a large pot. Slowly pour the milk into this mixture. Add crab meat and cook at medium heat 5 minutes.
- Add cream, stir and remove from heat before soup reaches full boil.
- Add sherry and Worcestershire sauce.
- Serve very hot.

Makes 6 servings

Mary Lincoln's Scalloped Oysters

Abraham Lincoln seems to have taken little notice of food, but he would always eat oysters...in any form. Mary Todd Lincoln used this recipe to tempt her husband to eat more often.

¼ cup melted butter
2 cups coarse cracker crumbs
2 dozen oysters, drained (reserve liquid)
⅓ cup cream
2 tbsp sherry
¼ tsp coarse black pepper
1 tsp Worcestershire sauce

- Mix melted butter and cracker crumbs.
- Sprinkle a third of mixture evenly on bottom of greased, shallow baking dish and add layer of oysters.
- Stir together cream, oyster liquid, sherry, pepper and Worcestershire sauce; pour half of sauce mixture over oysters.
- Add one-third more of butter and crumb mixture to baking dish, place remaining oysters on top and add remaining sauce.
- Sprinkle rest of crumb mixture on top and bake at 425° for 10 or 15 minutes until crumbs are lightly browned.

Makes 6 servings

Eleanor Roosevelt's Kedgeree

Like many women of her class and era, Eleanor Roosevelt never really learned to cook. However, she was famous for her "chafing-dish scrambled egg" suppers. This New England Kedgeree was also popular with family and friends.

2 cups cooked flaked seafood (white fish, crab meat, salmon, tuna, etc.)
2 cups cooked rice
½ cup milk or cream
4 tbsp melted butter
dash salt, dash pepper
4 hard-boiled eggs, sliced, chopped, or quartered

- Mix flaked fish and rice together, moistening with milk or cream.
- Sauté gently in melted butter.
- Add salt, pepper and hard-boiled eggs.
- Spoon mixture lightly (do not pack down) into 1-quart casserole.
- Cook 15 minutes at 325° or until piping hot and slightly browned.

Makes 6 servings

Jackie Kennedy's Chicken in White Wine

Jackie Kennedy was one of most accomplished hostesses in White House history. Her meals were equally famous for the conversation, the clothes, and the cuisine. This recipe is a good example of the latter.

4 tbsp butter
¼ pound chopped salt pork
¾ cups chopped white onion
1 sliced carrot
1 minced garlic clove
2 minced shallots
3 pounds of chicken white meat
2 tbsp flour
2 tbsp chopped fresh parsley
1 tsp marjoram
½ bay leaf
½ tsp thyme
2 cups white wine
¾ pound of sliced mushrooms
1 tsp salt
1 tsp pepper

- Melt the butter in a Dutch oven or covered pot.
- Add salt pork, onions, carrots, garlic and shallots. Brown these ingredients slightly.
- Remove the vegetables from the pan.
  - Brown the chicken in the residue in the pot.
    - Remove the chicken and use the same pot to stir together flour, parsley, marjoram, bay leaf, thyme, salt, and pepper.
      - As you stir, add the wine slowly.
    - Return the chicken to the pot and reduce the fire to low.
- Simmer for one hour.
- Return the vegetable mixture to the pot for the final ten minutes of cooking time.
- Add the mushrooms.
- Add salt and pepper to taste.
- Put the chicken on a platter and pour the sauce over it.

Makes 6-8 servings

Lady Bird Johnson's Pedernales River Chili

Lyndon and Lady Bird Johnson brought their own Texas traditions to the White House. Mrs. Johnson was an extraordinarily generous woman, who shared this special Texas recipe with family and friends.

4 lbs chuck, coarsely ground
2 small onions, chopped
2-3 cloves garlic, crushed
2 tsp salt
1 tsp oregano
1 tsp cumin seed
2 one-lb cans tomatoes, mashed
  slightly
2 tbsp chili powder
2 cups hot water
2 one-lb, four-oz cans kidney beans
  (optional)
2-6 dashes of hot pepper sauce

- Lightly brown beef, onions and garlic.
- Add salt, oregano, cumin seed, tomatoes and chili powder.
- Pour the hot water over all and mix thoroughly.
- Add kidney beans and/or hot sauce if desired.
- Simmer uncovered over low heat about an hour, skimming fat frequently.
- Serve hot at once, or store in refrigerator several days and reheat.

Makes 2½–3 quarts or 12 servings

Abigail Adams' Floating Island

John and Abigail Adams opened the White House to the public for the first time on New Year's Day in 1801. They served Floating Island, a show-stopping entertainment treat!

5 egg yolks
5 egg whites
1 quart milk
8 tbsp sugar
dash of vanilla extract
  (optional)
⅛ tsp salt

- Beat egg yolks together with one egg white.
- Scald milk and stir a little into the egg mixture to prevent curdling, then add rest of milk and 5 tablespoons of the sugar.
- Cook over low fire until thickened. Remove from heat, cool and flavor with vanilla if desired.
- Pour custard into bowl and chill.
- Add salt to remaining 4 egg whites and whip until frothy, adding remaining 3 tablespoons of sugar.
- Pour froth onto a shallow dish of boiling water to allow steam-cooking of meringue.
- When firm, drop the meringue a tablespoonful at a time on the custard far enough apart so that "islands" do not touch.
- Serve cold. You may also pour custard into individual cups, dropping an "island" on top of each.

Makes 6-8 servings

Dolley Madison's Soft Gingerbread

Dolley Madison is the undisputed greatest First Lady. After her husband died, she moved back to Washington and continued to be at the center of every social event until her death in 1849. This soft gingerbread was one of her specialties.

1 cup molasses
⅔ cup fresh beef drippings
¼ cup hot water
1 cup very hot water
2¼ cups flour
1 rounded tsp baking soda
1 rounded tbsp ground ginger
1 tbsp ground cinnamon
powdered sugar

- Mix molasses and beef drippings.
- Dissolve baking soda in the ¼ cup of hot water and add to molasses and drippings mixture.
- Sift together flour, ginger and cinnamon and add alternately with the cup of very hot water to molasses and drippings mixture.
- Beat well until batter is thoroughly mixed and soft enough to pour.
- Bake in shallow, well-greased pan at 350° for 30 to 40 minutes, or until center of cake springs back when pressed gently.
- Serve warm, sprinkled with powdered sugar.

Makes 6 servings

Edith Roosevelt's Sagamore Hill Sand Tarts

These special cookies were offered to anyone who dropped in on the
Roosevelt Family on Christmas Day at Sagamore Hill. Teddy loved them!

1 cup butter
2 cups sugar
3 eggs (separate white of one egg)
2 tsp vanilla
4 cups sifted flour
dash of cinnamon
dash of sugar

- Cream together butter and sugar.
- Beat in eggs one by one and add vanilla.
- Add flour and mix well.
- Roll thin, cut into small cakes and brush
  surface of each with remaining egg
  white.
- Sprinkle with dash of cinnamon and
  pinch of sugar.
- Bake at 350° for 8 minutes.

Makes 6 dozen

Bess Truman's Ozark Pudding

Bess Truman was described as a
"lady unchanged by the White
House and determined to remain
always what she is." She worked
hard at her duties and was well-
respected for her gracious charm.
This is her favorite dessert.

1 egg, well-beaten
¾ cup sugar
3 tbsp flour
1¼ tsp baking powder
⅛ tsp salt
½ cup chopped nuts
1 tsp vanilla
½ cup pared and chopped apples

- Add sugar gradually to well-beaten egg
  until mixture is very smooth.
- Sift flour, baking powder and salt.
- Blend the dry ingredients into egg and
  sugar mixture and stir in vanilla.
- Fold in nuts and apples and stir well.
- Pour into buttered 9-inch pie plate or
  1-quart casserole.
- Bake at 350° for 20 to 25 minutes.
- Serve with ice cream or whipped cream
  to which dash of sugar and 1 tablespoon
  of rum has been added.

Makes 6 servings

Mamie Eisenhower's "Million-Dollar" Fudge

Mamie Eisenhower always served frozen vegetables at the White House because they were the latest technological marvel. She also made what she called "Million-Dollar Fudge." (Back in those days, a million dollars was a lot of money!)

4 ½ cups sugar
¼ tsp salt
2 tbsp butter
1 14 oz can evaporated milk
12 oz sweet German chocolate
12 oz semisweet chocolate bits
1 pint marshmallow creme
2 cups chopped nuts

- Combine the first four ingredients in a large pot.
- Bring to a boil. Allow to boil for 6 minutes.
- Add in the remaining ingredients, stirring constantly.
- Beat until the chocolate has melted completely and the mixture is smooth.
- Pour mixture into a buttered glass dish.
- Allow to cool before slicing into squares.

Makes 30 squares

Hillary Rodham Clinton's Chocolate Chip Cookies

During the 1992 campaign, Hillary Rodham Clinton was criticized because she said she had not *"stayed home and baked cookies and had teas."* A "cookie bakeoff" was arranged between Mrs. Clinton and Barbara Bush. (This recipe by Clinton won by ten percentage points.)

1 cup solid vegetable shortening
½ cup granulated sugar
1 cup firmly packed light brown sugar
1 tsp vanilla
2 eggs
1½ cups unsifted all-purpose flour
1 tsp salt
1 tsp baking soda
2 cups rolled oats
1 package (12 oz) semi-sweet chocolate chips

- Grease several baking sheets. Preheat oven to 350 degrees.
- Beat shortening, sugar, and vanilla in a large bowl until creamy.
- Add eggs, beating until light and fluffy.
- Combine flour, salt, and baking soda in a separate bowl.
- Gradually add flour mixture to the egg mixture, beating constantly.
- Add rolled oats.
- Stir in chocolate chips.
- Drop batter in heaping teaspoonsful onto the greased baking sheet.
- Bake 8 to 10 minutes or until golden.
- Leave cookies on baking sheets for 2 minutes on wire racks. Then remove cookies to wire rack to finish cooling completely.

Makes about 4 dozen cookies